330.01   9059300

Between Marginalism and Marxism

Between Marginalism and Marxism
The economic sociology of J.A. Schumpeter

TOM BOTTOMORE

HARVESTER
WHEATSHEAF

New York London Toronto Sydney Tokyo Singapore

First published 1992 by
Harvester Wheatsheaf,
Campus 400, Maylands Avenue
Hemel Hempstead
Hertfordshire HP2 7EZ
A division of
Simon & Schuster International Group

© 1992 Tom Bottomore
The right of Tom Bottomore to be identified as the author of this work has been asserted by him in accordance with the Copyright, Design and Patents Act of 1988.

All rights reserved. No part of this publication may be reproduced, stored in a retrieval system, or transmitted, in any form, or by any means, electronic, mechanical, photocopying, recording or otherwise, without prior permission, in writing, from the publisher.

Typeset in 10/12pt Times
by Photoprint, Torquay, Devon

Printed and bound in Great Britain by
Biddles Ltd, Guildford and King's Lynn

British Library Cataloguing in Publication Data

A catalogue record for this book is available from the British Library.

ISBN 0–7450–0182–3

1 2 3 4 5   96 95 94 93 92

For Katherine, Stephen and Eleanor

CONTENTS

Introduction 1
Chapter 1   Formative influences 5
Chapter 2   Methodological peregrinations 15
Chapter 3   The theory of economic development 28
Chapter 4   Sociological excursions 45
Chapter 5   Economic cycles 62
Chapter 6   Capitalist development and decline 85
Chapter 7   Socialism and democracy 101
Chapter 8   The realm of economic sociology 112
Bibliography 137
Index 147

INTRODUCTION

Schumpeter began his *History of Economic Analysis* (1954) with an examination of the scope and method of economics, its relation to other sciences, and the extent to which it is influenced by ideological conceptions. In his view, the 'scientific' economist can be distinguished from others who write about economic matters by a command of four fundamental techniques of analysis. The first of these is economic history, of which Schumpeter wrote that it 'is by far the most important', and that if he were beginning his work in economics anew and could choose only one field of study, this would be his choice. He asserted its importance on three grounds: (i) that 'the subject matter of economics is essentially a unique process in historic time', and 'nobody can hope to understand the economic phenomena of any . . . epoch who has not an adequate command of historical *facts* and an adequate amount of historical *sense*'; (ii) 'the historical report cannot be purely economic but must inevitably reflect also "institutional facts"', and hence 'affords the best method for understanding how economic and non-economic facts *are* related to one another'; and (iii) 'that most of the fundamental errors currently committed in economic analysis are due to lack of historical experience more often than to any other shortcoming' (pp. 12–13).[1]

A second technique is that of statistics, which is vitally important not only for explaining things but also in order to know precisely what there is to explain.

'Theory' is the third fundamental field, comprising explanatory hypotheses, and – which Schumpeter considered more important –

models and axioms (or principles), as 'instruments or tools framed for the purpose of *establishing* interesting results'. They are complemented by other 'gadgets' – 'concepts, relations between concepts, and methods of handling these relations' – 'the sum total of such gadgets' constituting economic theory. Schumpeter summed up his view by citing the 'unsurpassably felicitous phrase' of Joan Robinson that 'economic theory is a box of tools' (p. 15).

Finally, Schumpeter distinguished a fourth field, economic sociology, which he considered just as important as economic history; for the latter is not alone in providing the institutional framework within which the schemata of economic theory are supposed to function.

> It is easy to see that when we introduce the institutions of private property or of free contracting or else a greater or smaller amount of government regulation, we are introducing social facts that are not simply economic history but are a sort of generalized or typified or stylized economic history. And this applies still more to the general forms of human behaviour which we assume either in general or for certain social situations but not for others. (p. 20)

In this book I shall be concerned, first, to examine the social and intellectual environment in which Schumpeter formed his conception of economic analysis, and secondly, to consider how far he did adopt a historical and sociological approach in his major writings, not merely in those – such as the monographs on imperialism (1919) and social classes (1927), or his work on capitalism, socialism and democracy (1942) – which are most explicitly sociological, but throughout his work. The first part of this enquiry involves looking at the milieu, in Vienna, and more widely in Germany and the Habsburg Empire, at the beginning of the twentieth century when Schumpeter embarked on his studies: a milieu in which there were intense debates about the methodology of the social sciences; acute political conflicts accompanying the rapid spread of socialism and nationalism; a wide diffusion of Marxist thought, and notably the emergence of a distinctive Austro-Marxist school; a continuing development of Austrian marginal utility theory in economics, directed to a large extent against Marxism; and a significant expansion of sociology, related in some aspects to the work of the German historical school in economics, and closely involved with economic questions in the work of Max Weber and the Austro-Marxists.

Following this preliminary account of the context of Schumpeter's thought, the major part of my study is devoted to a critical examination of his own writings on methodology, and his analyses of economic development, business cycles, capitalism and socialism, to determine how far he did employ a consistent method and succeed in connecting economic, historical and sociological facts in his interpretation of social trends. There can be no doubt, at all events, that throughout his life he was primarily interested in the processes of economic and social development, and these preoccupations created a certain affinity between his own thought and Marxism, as he himself recognized. But Schumpeter also conceived his work as a critique of Marxist conceptions, from an economic and sociological perspective, and it was undertaken in a spirit akin to that which informed many of Max Weber's writings, though on the basis of a much more profound knowledge of Marxist thought and the socialist movement. One important element in the present book, therefore, is a comparison between the ideas, theoretical models and analyses of Schumpeter and Marx (the latter especially in their Austro-Marxist form), and a consideration of how Marxists might in turn criticize Schumpeter or on the other hand find in his work conceptions which would amplify, refine and correct their own interpretations.

During the past two decades Schumpeter's work has come very much into fashion, attracting wider attention than perhaps at any previous time; and as Hutchison (1982) remarked in comparing the influence of Schumpeter and Keynes, 'in the 1980s, for an allegedly almost chronically crisis-ridden subject, perhaps Schumpeter's work, and his style as an economist, have more to offer'. By far the greater part of recent writing, however, has concentrated almost exclusively on Schumpeter's contributions as an economist, and this particular emphasis needs, I think, to be corrected, not least in the light of his own declared predilections. My aim in this book is to bring into greater prominence the underlying scheme of sociological and historical ideas which informed Schumpeter's studies, and in the concluding chapter to suggest ways in which we can derive from it some of the important elements that are needed for the construction of a new economic sociology (or sociological economics) which, drawing upon both Schumpeter and Marx, as well as on Max Weber, would acquire a far more influential place in the social sciences.

Note

1. Schumpeter added, as a comment on this passage, that 'since history is an important source . . . of the economist's material and since, moreover, the economist himself is a product of his own *and all preceding* time, economic analysis and its results are certainly affected by historical relativity'. This view led him to pay particular attention to the influence of what he called 'the spirit of the times' and the politics of each period, on the development of economic analysis.

CHAPTER 1

FORMATIVE INFLUENCES

Vienna, in the period from the last decade of the nineteenth century to the First World War, was the scene of a prodigious outburst of cultural and intellectual creativity in many different spheres – in art and architecture, literature, music, philosophy, psychology and the social sciences. This creative upsurge was indeed part of a more general European movement,[1] which embraced modernism in the arts and the spread of new styles of philosophical thought (neo-Kantianism in various forms, positivism and its diverse critics), but it found a particularly concentrated expression in Vienna[2] and was associated with major social changes in the Habsburg Empire, where rapid industrialization and urbanization[3] produced new and sharper class divisions, an increasingly powerful socialist movement, alongside which nationalist movements also flourished,[4] and mounting criticism of the resistance to change of what appeared increasingly a doomed imperial system.

In literature the contradictory character of a society in which the traditional modes of expression and forms of behaviour had lost their meaning was most vividly and critically depicted by Karl Kraus and Robert Musil. Kraus – described by Barea (1966, p. 261) as 'the implacable prosecutor of all that was rotten in the state of Austria and in Vienna' – waged a life-long campaign (extending into the 1930s)[5] against the moral and intellectual debasement of the German language: 'In every single case his field of action is the ever-widening no-man's-land between appearance and reality, expression and substance, word-gesture and personality' (Heller 1952, p. 237). The same no-man's-land is portrayed in Musil's description of 'Kakania' on the eve of the First World War[6] as a state which on paper

> called itself the Austro-Hungarian Monarchy; in speaking, however, one referred to it as Austria, that is to say, it was known by a name that it had, as a State, solemnly renounced by oath . . . By its constitution it was liberal, but its system of government was clerical. . . . Before the law all citizens were equal, but not everyone, of course, was a citizen. There was a parliament, which made such vigorous use of its liberty that it was usually kept shut, but there was also an emergency powers act by means of which it was possible to manage without Parliament. . . . Many such things happened in this State.

Alongside this kind of critique of language, and in some cases influenced by it, a systematic philosophy of language was developed by Mauthner and subsequently by Wittgenstein, while in another direction a philosophy of science was expounded in different forms by Mach, Boltzmann, Hertz and the Vienna Circle (see Janik and Toulmin 1973, Chapter 5). These two streams of philosophical thought, arising from neo-Kantian and positivist reflections on how the external reality of nature and society could be adequately represented in language, and also from the increasing practical importance of science and technology in social life, were fresh attempts, in the words of Janik and Toulmin (1973, p. 146), 'to define the scope, conditions of validity, and boundaries of different media, symbolisms, modes of expression and/or languages.'[7] It may be added that in Vienna there was a unique sensibility to the limits of particular languages and symbolisms, because the massive immigration brought together individuals from all over the Empire, producing a polyglot and cosmopolitan community in which cultural diversity helped to stimulate creativity, but was also the source of tensions between national and ethnic groups.[8]

This milieu manifestly influenced Schumpeter's own intellectual development, in specific as well as more diffuse ways. But he was also affected by the circumstances of his early life, during which he may be said to have inhabited two quite different worlds. As the son of a textile manufacturer he belonged to a family of the new wealthy bourgeoisie, but his father died when Schumpeter was four years old, and six years later his mother married as her second husband an aristocrat, Field Marshal-Lieutenant Sigmund von Kéler. Schumpeter then entered a different social sphere, and in 1893 he became a scholar at an exclusive school for the sons of the aristocracy, the Theresianum.[9] The influence of these two worlds on Schumpeter's character and outlook was suggested in a memorial tribute by Smithies (1951, pp. 16–17):

> He adopted the manners, the habits, and the tastes of the aristocrat. ... But he must have realized that conspicuous success in the normal aristocratic pursuits – the diplomatic service or the army – was unlikely, and, besides, they would not afford him the intellectual life he demanded. ... He therefore had to strike out on a line of his own.[10]

In the event Schumpeter did follow his own path, in a way which both satisfied his intellectual ambitions and brought him eventually into close contact again with the business world. He entered the University of Vienna in 1901 as a student of law and economics, evincing a growing interest in the latter field, though without neglecting the study of law (which he briefly practised later, in 1907–8). At that time there already existed a distinctive 'Austrian' school of economics (often referred to in Austria as the 'Viennese' school), notwithstanding the differences of view that emerged as the original ideas of Menger (1871) were developed by Wieser and Böhm-Bawerk.[11] What distinguished the school was, first, a strong commitment to economics as a theoretical science, which brought Menger in particular into conflict with the historical school of economics then dominant in Germany; secondly, the exposition of a theory of value and price in terms of the relation between individuals and useful, scarce objects (in due course known as 'marginal utility' theory after Wieser (1893) introduced this expression), which substituted subjective valuations and choices for inherent properties of the object (as in the labour theory of value); and thirdly, the extension of the theory by Wieser to interpret costs as sacrificed utilities ('opportunity costs') and to determine the value of factors of production, embodied in the final product, by 'imputation', and by Böhm-Bawerk to a theory of interest based on subjective valuations of present and future goods.

The theoretical ideas of the Austrian economists were developed in the intellectual environment that I have described, in which neo-Kantian and positivist philosophies were powerful influences. Menger, as appears from his book on methodology (1883), was a positivist in several senses: in the emphasis which he laid on economic laws and prediction, and on the similarities between the social and natural sciences. But he was not a thoroughgoing empiricist. He made a distinction between 'exact' laws (in principle untestable by empirical methods) and 'empirical' laws (which can be so tested and may be falsified), assigning primacy to the former as the core of economics as an exact science. It remains unclear, however, whether these exact laws can be tested at all (if not by empirical, then by logical methods) and how they are established in the first place, though Menger seems to suggest that they derive from some initial assumptions about human behaviour.[12] Böhm-Bawerk, on the other hand, held empiricist views and maintained that the 'abstract-deductive method . . . has no fancy *a priori* axioms as a basis for its inferences' but, like the historical school, starts 'with observations of actual conditions and endeavours from this empirical material to construct general laws' (1924, p. 263). Wieser, however, developed Menger's notion of 'exact laws', while emphasizing the difference between the social and natural sciences insofar as the former could make use of 'inner observation' or introspection and by this means establish necessary propositions concerning human behaviour. From this standpoint he criticized Schumpeter (and implicitly Menger) for being 'blinded by the success of the exact natural sciences' (Wieser 1929, p. 12.).

Whether Schumpeter was a positivist in this strong sense will be considered further in the next chapter, but it is clear that like other Austrians at that time he was much influenced by positivist ideas, and this showed itself, in his later writings, in the distinctions he made between science and ideology, positive science and metaphysics,[13] and more generally between a realm of facts and a realm of values (in much the same manner as Max Weber, with whose writings he was very familiar). But he was also influenced by neo-Kantian conceptions of the role of the knowing subject in the constitution of knowledge that were conducive to the construction of models defining the scope and conditions of validity of economics as a science (see above, page 6). Menger's 'exact laws', insofar as they rest upon assumptions about human behaviour, or as expounded by Wieser derive from introspection or self-reflection, conform to this neo-Kantian approach; and Schumpeter, as we shall see, strongly emphasized the importance of models, as against explanatory hypotheses, in the development of economic theory.

There was another major source from which Schumpeter imbibed positivist and neo-Kantian views, namely the Austro-Marxist thinkers.[14] He became familiar with their ideas, and with Marxist thought generally, during his student years, but particularly in 1905–6 when he took part in a seminar conducted by Böhm-Bawerk which became famous for the exceptionally lively character of its discussions, involving on one side a group of young Marxist thinkers – among them Emil Lederer, Otto Neurath, Rudolf Hilferding and Otto Bauer – and on the other side the proponents of marginal utility theory, including Böhm-Bawerk himself and the youthful Ludwig von Mises, who later became one of the fiercest critics of Marxism and socialism (Mises 1920, 1922).[15] At this time Hilferding (1904) had just published his critique of Böhm-Bawerk[16] which provided a general framework for Marxist criticism of 'subjective' or 'psychological' value theory,[17] and Schumpeter thus encountered very early in his career two clearly formulated and opposed conceptions of economic theory, which remained present in his thought throughout his life.[18]

This, however, was not all that Schumpeter acquired from his association with the Austro-Marxists.[19] It is evident that the dominant theme in Schumpeter's major writings is the economic development of capitalism as a social system, which is also, of course, the principal theme of Marxist theory; so that in many respects, including the use of a particular terminology, there is a significant affinity between the two approaches. To be sure, there were also other intellectual sources of Schumpeter's special interest in capitalist development, among them notably the writings of the German historical school, and in particular those of Schmoller, Sombart and Weber (Schumpeter 1954, pp. 807–24).[20] It may be argued indeed that the three outstanding theorists of the development of modern capitalism – Marx, Weber and Schumpeter – were all economic sociologists,[21] whose basic conceptions were related in some ways, while diverging in others.

Here it should be noted that one major respect in which Schumpeter diverged from Marxist thought was in his commitment, especially marked in his earlier years, to the views of the Austrian school, complemented by those of Walras, whose equilibrium analysis he always valued highly; and in accordance with these views he adopted intially a 'subjective' approach, or what he called, in his first book (1908), 'methodological individualism'. There was a wider sense too in which individualism was an important element in his thought, both in his account of capitalist development, in which the entrepreneur as a creative, innovating individual plays a central role, and in his later discussion of democracy in terms of political leadership (1942). The idea of the importance of creative individuals in the economic process Schumpeter imbibed in the first place from his teacher, Wieser; but along with that he also assimilated the conception of impersonal historical forces, and in consequence there was always present in his thought, as in Wieser's, a tension between alternative methodological orientations which will be examined in the next chapter.

After graduating from the University of Vienna in February 1906 Schumpeter proceeded to extend his knowledge of contemporary economic theory by going first to Berlin for the summer semester as a participant in the political economy seminar, and then as a research student to the London School of Economics, making frequent visits to Oxford and Cambridge. While in England he married an Englishwoman, and in 1907 they went to Cairo where Schumpeter practised as a lawyer at the International Mixed Court until 1908 (Seidl 1984, pp. 190–1). During this very active period of travel, research and legal practice, he nevertheless wrote and published his first book *(Das Wesen und der Hauptinhalt der theoretischen Nationalökonomie*, 1908, referred to hereafter as *Das Wesen)*, which was conceived as a contribution 'to the epistemology of our science' (pp. 117–18) in the aftermath of the *Methodenstreit*, on the basis of all that Schumpeter had learned during the preceding seven years from his exposure to diverse conceptions of the capitalist economy, of economic theory and method, of the place of historical and sociological studies in economic analysis, and of the scope and validity of theoretical models and explanations as expounded in the new philosophies of science. This provides, therefore, the starting-point for a systematic examination, in the next chapter, of Schumpeter's own methodology as it was stated or implied in the course of his subsequent studies.

Notes

1. See the observations by Csáky (1986, p. 140) who points to the influence of other centres such as Paris, Berlin and Munich.
2. There is a substantial and growing literature on Viennese cultural life at the turn of the century, among which the general studies by Janik and Toulmin (1973), Schorske (1980), and Berner, Brix and Mantl (1986) are especially valuable.
3. During the second half of the nineteenth century, and particularly in the 1890s, the Habsburg Empire was transformed from a mainly agricultural to an industrial state where a quarter of the population (and in some regions almost a half) was employed in manufacture. The total population itself increased from 30 million to 50 million, while in Vienna it quadrupled from half a million to more than 2 million by 1910. A study of Vienna from the eighteenth century to 1914 by Ilsa Barea (1966) gives an exceptionally good account (Chapters 5 and 6) of the impact of the economic and social changes from the 1860s onwards on politics and cultural life, and the accelerating decay of the imperial system.
4. It was in response to this situation that Otto Bauer produced his study of social democracy and the national question (1907), which is still today the outstanding Marxist work in this field and a major contribution to the analysis of nation states and nationalism. For excerpts from Bauer's book, and a discussion of this and the related studies by Karl Renner (1899, 1902), see Bottomore and Goode (1978); and see also Nimni (1991, Chapters 5–7).
5. In his literary–political review *Die Fackel* (founded in 1899) and in his drama *Die letzten Tage der Menschheit (The Last Days of Humanity)*.
6. In the first volume of *The Man Without Qualities*, pp. 32–3.
7. They also raised particular problems concerning the foundations of morality, and of value systems in general, which preoccupied, in different ways, Wittgenstein (see Janik and Toulmin 1973, Chapter 6) and Musil, both influenced by Tolstoy, as they did also Max Weber, the Austro-Marxists and to some extent Schumpeter himself.
8. Further more, since a relatively high proportion of the immigrants were Jewish, this was also fertile ground for the growth of anti-Semitism (see Pulzer 1986).
9. See Seidl (1984, p. 190) who speculates that the principal reason which led Mrs Schumpeter, who was independently wealthy, to marry a man who was 33 years older than herself (and from whom she later separated, in 1906) was perhaps her desire to open the doors of Viennese society to her son, for whom she was always extremely ambitious. For a full account of Schumpeter's life see Swedberg (1991).

10. Schumpeter, according to several commentators, retained a certain nostalgia for the old Habsburg Empire, and as his later Harvard colleagues remarked 'he remained to the end the cultivated Austrian gentleman of the old school who had seen everything but who found in the succession of events since 1914 no very striking evidence of progress' (Harris 1951, p. ix). This may account for the somewhat detached and sceptical (even disabused) view of the civilization of industrial capitalism which is discernible in some of his later writings.
11. See Hutchison (1981, Chapters 6 and 7) and the further discussion in Chapter 2 below.
12. For a more detailed, and on some points divergent, account of Menger's methodology, see Milford 1990.
13. Thus he says, in praise of Marx, that 'nowhere did he betray positive science to metaphysics' (1942, p. 9).
14. Max Adler, in numerous writings, expounded the principles of a Marxist science of society (sociology) based upon a concept of 'socialized humanity' or 'social association' which is regarded as being 'transcendentally given as a category of knowledge' (Adler 1925; see also Adler 1904, and the Introduction and translations in Bottomore and Goode 1978). This provided a theoretical and methodological framework which was broadly accepted by other Austro-Marxists and played a major part in forming the distinctive outlook of the school.
15. Nevertheless, Mises (1978) later gave a generous account of these seminar debates in his memoirs: 'It was a great day in the history of the University of Vienna and in the development of political economy when Böhm began his seminar. As the theme for the first semester Böhm chose the principles of the theory of value. Otto Bauer set out from a Marxist standpoint to dismember subjective value theory. The discussion between Bauer and Böhm – the other participants remained in the background – occupied the whole winter semester. Bauer's brilliant talents were luminously displayed, and he showed himself a worthy opponent of the great master whose critique of Marxist political economy had delivered a *coup de grâce*' (translated from the text cited by Mozetič 1987, p. 38).
16. In which he argued that Marx's theory of value rests upon a conception of 'society' and 'social relations', whereas the marginalist theory begins from individuals. From a Marxist standpoint 'the object of political economy is the social aspect of the commodity, of the good, in so far as it is a symbol of social interconnection', whereas 'the representative of the psychological school of political economy [Böhm-Bawerk] fails to see this social nexus' and 'starts from the individual relationships of human beings with each other'. Hilferding's text expounds in a strong form a view of political economy as

Formative influences 13

economic sociology within a Marxist system of sociology, as do many of his later writings, and I shall examine it further in due course.

17. However, the Marxist participants in Böhm-Bawerk's seminar themselves had differing attitudes to the marginal utility theory. While Hilferding rejected it completely, Bauer and Lederer were more inclined to look for some synthesis of the Marxist and subjective value theories (see Mozetič 1987, p. 95, and his general discussion of the Austro-Marxist responses, pp. 95–111). Neurath, who was closely associated with the Austro-Marxists as well as being a principal founder of the Vienna Circle, later expounded an idiosyncratic, strictly positivist and 'physicalist' version of Marxist sociology (Neurath 1931) and also developed a theory of a 'natural' economy (Neurath 1920; see Bottomore 1990, pp. 24–5) which was totally opposed to the ideas of the marginal utility school. His contributions to the seminar were dismissed by Mises as 'nonsense' (Mozetič 1987, p. 107–21).

18. This will be seen in later chapters. But Schumpeter never undertook any substantial critical appraisal of the Austro-Marxist positions from his own standpoint, even though he was clearly influenced by them in his studies of Marxism and of capitalist development. His comment (Schumpeter 1954, p. 881) that 'Hilferding . . . wrote a notable reply to Böhm-Bawerk's criticism of Marx and other things, which a fuller review could not pass by' is fairly representative of the brevity of his direct references.

19. His relations with Bauer and Hilferding appear to have remained fairly close and friendly, as is suggested by the fact that he was invited to act as a consultant to the German Commission on Socialization (of which Hilferding was a leading member) and participated in its work from January to March 1919, when he was appointed Secretary of the Treasury in the coalition government of the new Austrian Republic (apparently proposed by Bauer) and remained in this post until October 1919. Later still, he wrote sympathetically of Hilferding's problems as finance minister in the German government formed in June 1928: 'We now have a socialist minister who faces the exceptionally difficult task of curing or improving a situation bequeathed by non-socialist financial policies' (Schumpeter 1928a).

20. Schumpeter (1954, p. 816) assigned Weber to what he called 'the youngest historical school', and while observing that Weber was 'not really an economist at all', noted that 'his work and teaching had much to do with the emergence of Economic Sociology in the sense of an analysis of economic institutions, the recognition of which as a distinct field clarified so many "methodological" issues' (p. 819). Schumpeter's familiarity with Weber's writings is evident from in-

direct references and similarities of approach, as well as criticisms, which I shall consider later, and he was associated with Weber both as a contributor to the *Archiv für Sozialwissenschaft und Sozialpolitik* and as a member of the editorial board of the collection *Grundriss der Sozialökonomik*.
21. See Bottomore (1985).

CHAPTER 2

METHODOLOGICAL PEREGRINATIONS

Reflections on methodology, and more broadly on epistemology and scientific method, are to be found throughout Schumpeter's writings, but he also wrote a number of studies specifically concerned with these topics. Indeed, his first published article (1906), on mathematical methods in economic theory, and his first book (*Das Wesen*, 1908), on the nature and content of theoretical economics, were devoted to an analysis of methods and of some wider issues raised by the philosophy of science. The sources upon which he drew in these works were the ideas of the Austrian school as propounded by Menger, and in the second generation by Böhm-Bawerk and Wieser; the famous *Methodenstreit* of the 1880s which had opposed economists over the choice between a mainly logical–deductive method (Menger) and a mainly historical–inductive method (Schmoller);[1] the debate between Marxists and adherents of the Austrian school in Böhm-Bawerk's seminar of 1905–6 (see above, page 9), which encompassed some issues that were similar to those raised by the economists of the historical school; and his own assimilation, during the period of his university studies and subsequent research in Germany and England, of a wide range of different styles of economic analysis, including notably the equilibrium analysis of Walras and the writings of the British economists.[2]

In his article of 1906 Schumpeter made a case for the use of mathematical methods (or techniques) in theoretical economics, countered some objections to it, and described briefly the major contributions by Cournot, Jevons, Walras, Pareto, Marshall and

Edgeworth; and much later, in his *History* (1954, pp. 954–63), he presented a substantially similar account, noting the important contribution that mathematics had made to 'pure theory' during the past half-century, including the development of econometrics. Curiously, however, in his discussion of what he called the techniques of economic analysis at the beginning of the *History* (pp. 12–24), he referred to 'statistics' (not mathematics) as a principal technique, and, in discussing 'theory', as another major technique he concentrated on the use of explanatory hypotheses, concepts and models, without mentioning mathematics. Furthermore, a third technique, that of economic history (closely associated with economic sociology) was now declared to be 'by far the most important' (*ibid.*, p. 12). It is difficult, therefore, to accept without substantial qualification the view of Machlup (1951, pp. 95–6) that there was no evolution in Schumpeter's thought 'from the youthful keenness of a mathematical turn of mind to the mature perspective of a historical one', or that his work can be adequately described as manifesting a deliberate 'methodological tolerance' rather than a somewhat 'weak eclecticism' which allowed him to pursue diverse enquiries without too much concern for the overall consistency of his approach, or its relation to other orientations and models in economic theory.

We can begin to clarify this question by looking at the methodological treatise (*Das Wesen*) with which he began his career. Its aim, as he stated in the preface (p. xii), was to develop, or at least contribute to, an 'epistemology of economics', tacitly conceived in terms of the prevailing philosophies of science (see above, page 6) as defining the scope, conditions of validity, and limits, of economics as a theoretical social science.[3] But he then introduced into the prefatory exposition of his intention a number of specific issues which detract somewhat from the unity of economics as a science. Thus he expressed in general terms the idea of methodological 'tolerance', particularly with reference to the *Methodenstreit* (p. xiv; and see also n. 1), of which he says that it was a case where different principles of method, regarded as universally valid, were opposed to each other; unnecessarily in his view since the alternative methods should be considered in relation to each other, specifying the scope and limits of each. In the same context, Schumpeter refers to the opposition between deductive and inductive methods, which should be treated in a similar fashion.

The difficulty with this approach is that we are now presented, not with a single economic science, but with two (or more) which have their own distinct conditions of validity and limits. The matter is further complicated by another, related distinction which Schumpeter (p. xix) makes between 'static' and 'dynamic' analysis. The methods of 'pure theory' (by which is meant the marginal utility theory) are, he observes, as yet only adequate for static analysis, and he has little more to say about dynamic analysis, aside from a few brief comments at the end of the book (pp. 614–22) which seem to exclude it from the realm of theory and assign it to a sphere of historical–descriptive study. In his later work, of course, Schumpeter was primarily concerned with problems of economic development and social change, but in this first methodological work he declared that the central problem of economics is equilibrium analysis (p. xix), from which the theory of exchange, price, money and distribution is derived, and he indicated his own major allegiance to the conceptions of Walras and Wieser (p. ix).

The theme of methodological tolerance, or a permissible (indeed useful) eclecticism, is pursued in the introductory chapter where the development of 'modern' economic theory in the work of Jevons, Menger and Walras is seen as having its source in the classical school of Adam Smith, Ricardo and their immediate followers, whose work moreover retains an independent value and, as Schumpeter says, 'still lives' (p. 16). The development of economic theory and research is not, therefore, by any means a simple linear process, and Schumpeter went on (pp. 16–19) to distinguish three main 'schools' in recent theory – that which based itself on classical theory, the Austrians, and the group around Alfred Marshall – as well as several other research orientations, all of which contributed to the growth of economics as a science, though not in every case to its character as an 'exact' science.

There were, however, limits to Schumpeter's tolerance. At the end of his introduction (p. 20) he referred very briefly to the economic theory of what he chose to call 'scientific socialism' rather than Marxism, and said that it would be excluded from his discussion, though not through any hostility to socialism as such. On what grounds then was it excluded? By this date Marxist economic theory was already widely known and discussed, nowhere more so than in Austria where Schumpeter had a particularly close acquaintance with it through the writings of

Bauer and Hilferding, and through his participation in Böhm-Bawerk's seminar of 1905–6. Yet in all his writings Schumpeter's attitude to the Austro-Marxists remained curiously coy and ambiguous. On the one hand he praised their talents and achievements, while on the other he refrained from any serious examination of their work, even though he drew upon it to a large extent in later writings, notably in his discussion of Marxism and of the development of capitalism in *Capitalism, Socialism and Democracy* (1942). Thus, in a paragraph of his *History* (p. 881) which was indented and set in small type to indicate that it dealt with specialized issues outside the mainstream, he expressed his great regret at not being able to discuss the work of that 'brilliant man', Max Adler; or of Otto Bauer, 'a man of quite exceptional ability'; or of Rudolf Hilferding, who 'wrote a notable reply to Böhm-Bawerk's criticism of Marx' and 'was the author of the most famous performance of the neo-Marxist group: *Das Finanzkapital*'.

These compliments, however, are no substitute for a systematic assessment of a theoretical scheme which, during Schumpeter's lifetime, established itself as the principal alternative to the marginal utility theory, of which Schumpeter was in his own way an adherent, especially in his earlier years. But since Schumpeter himself did not make any such assessment we must do it for ourselves, and we can usefully begin by comparing the theoretical scheme and methodology which he outlined in Chapters 2–6 of *Das Wesen* (pp. 22–98) with the entirely different model set out by Hilferding (1904) in his critique of Böhm-Bawerk. Schumpeter's discussion in these chapters ranged over a variety of subjects, and I shall concentrate in the first place on those which are directly relevant to the present issue. He took as the starting-point of his theory the fact that we observe, in any kind of economy, economic subjects who possess determinate quantitites of determinate goods, and that all these 'economic quantities' stand in reciprocal relations of dependence on each other, so that a change in one of them brings about changes in others. Thus they 'form the elements of a system' (or model), the purpose of which is to describe more comprehensively and render more clearly intelligible the interconnection of the elements (i.e. the 'economic quantities'), so increasing our understanding (p. 42). Schumpeter then argued that when we set out to describe the relations between economic quantities we observe immediately an already constituted relationship, namely price, or the exchange relation (p. 49). This is therefore the focal point of economic analysis, and in a static analysis – or what he later called an analysis of the 'circular flow' – it involves an equilibrium model in which a change in one economic quantity produces compensating changes in others, which have further effects. This is of course a continuous process of adjustment and readjustment.

Schumpeter excluded from the conception of 'pure theory' expounded here any concern with how the actual distribution of economic quantities among subjects came to be established in the first place; or with the idea of the economy as a driving force in social life as a whole, such as was expressed in the classical theories and 'reached a culminating point in the so-called economic interpretation of history' (p. 51); or more generally with the dynamic, or developmental, aspects of the economy. He also differed from Menger in arguing that an analysis of, or assumptions about, the psychological dispositions of individuals were quite unnecessary as a basis for value theory (i.e. marginal utility theory), which rested on the simple observation of economic behaviour (p. 65). His own theoretical scheme, however, was focused in a different way on the actions of *individuals*, and he devoted a chapter of his book (pp. 88–98) to what he called 'methodological individualism' (a term which he seems to have originated, although the conception appears in Menger's writings). In the first part of his discussion he distinguished individualism as a method from the 'political' individualism which is opposed to socialism and to various forms of social policy intervention in the economy; the two are quite different and, he claimed, logically unrelated. Furthermore, he declared himself quite ready to accept the arguments of the historical school and of the advocates of a social policy approach concerning what the economy really is, and whether the individual or some other entity is its driving force; and he also agreed that social influences determine individual behaviour, while the single individual is an infinitesimal factor in the economic process. But all this, he argued, is irrelevant from the point of view of economic theory ('pure' or 'exact' theory). The important thing is how economic behaviour can best be 'schematized', i.e. constructed as a model, in order to achieve the practical result of gaining a clearer understanding of such behaviour (pp. 93–4). 'My aim is to describe specific and manifest economic transactions, and this within very narrow limits. The more profound causes underlying such transactions may be interesting, but they do not affect the results of my analysis. The investigation of them belongs to the field of sociology' (p. 94).

Hilferding's view of economic theory, succinctly expounded in his reply to Böhm-Bawerk (Hilferding 1904), was radically different. In the Marxist system, he observed, 'the analysis of the commodity constitutes the starting point' (p. 123), for 'the term commodity . . . is the expression of social relationships between mutually independent producers in so far as these relationships are effected through the instrumentality of goods. . . . The object of political economy is the social aspect of the commodity, of the good, in so far as it is a symbol of social interconnection' (p. 130). Thus, 'to the extent that labour in its social form becomes the measure of value, economics is established as a social and historical science' (p. 133). Hilferding then summarized his argument as follows:

> the [Marxist] law of value becomes a law of motion for a definite type of social organization based upon the production of commodities, for in the last resort all change in social structure can be referred to changes in the relationships of production, that is to say to changes in the evolution of productive power and in the organization of [productive] labour. We are thereby led, in the most striking contrast to the outlook of the psychological school, to regard political economy as a part of sociology, and sociology itself as a historical science. (p. 186)

Finally, 'the capitalist mode of production . . . socializes mankind to a greater extent than did any previous mode of production, that is to say, capitalism makes the existence of the individual man dependent upon the social relationships amid which he is placed', but 'it does so in an antagonistic form, by the establishment of the two great classes' (p. 190).

It is a very great loss to the history of economic thought that no record survives of the debate in Böhm-Bawerk's seminar of 1905–6, where, most unusually, two radically different conceptions of the nature and scope of economics as a social science came together in a profound and prolonged encounter. In the absence of such a record, and of any surviving notes, autobiographical material, or systematic studies by Schumpeter himself, relating to the issues raised in that debate, we have no direct way of knowing in precise detail how he responded to these exchanges, or what kind of influence they had upon his subsequent work. Indirectly, however, the influence of Marxist thought, mediated largely through the Austro-Marxists, can be shown by an examination of his changing approach to economic analysis, which became increasingly historical and sociological, focusing above all on economic development, the socialization of the economy, and the evolution of capitalism as a social system. At the same time, however, he continued to express, for many years, his high regard for the achievements of the Austrian marginal utility school and of Walras.

This apparently contradictory stance, which will be explored more fully in later chapters, illustrates very well the absence of one important element from Schumpeter's philosophy of science: namely, a conception of the progress of science through confrontation between rival theories, in which from time to time an established theory is replaced by an incompatible new one, in a process which may be interpreted as a sequence of 'conjectures' and 'refutations', or as a more broadly conceived 'paradigm-shift'.[4] It may be that progress of this kind is unattainable, or at any rate exceptionally difficult and uncertain, in the social sciences, where a multiplicity of coexisting paradigms (Masterman 1970, p. 74) seems to be the norm; but Schumpeter did not engage in any substantial discussion of these fundamental issues in his methodological writings, which are devoted for the most part to the narrower subject of techniques of research.

In the background of his writings, however, we can easily discern the influence of the two major currents of philosophical thought – positivism and neo-Kantianism – which played a significant part in forming the ideas of the Austrian school of economics and of the Austro-Marxists. There can be little doubt that Schumpeter was a positivist in several important senses of that protean term. At a later stage he defined 'modern' or 'empirical' or 'positive'[5] sciences by two principal characteristics: (i) 'they reduce the facts we are invited to accept *on scientific grounds* to the narrower category of "facts verifiable by observation or experiment"; and they reduce the range of admissible methods to "logical inference from verifiable facts" '; and (ii) 'Just as sciences grow by slow accretion when they have come into existence, so they emerge by slow accretion, gradually differentiating themselves, under the influence of favourable and inhibiting environmental and personal conditions, from their commonsense background and sometimes also from other sciences' (1954, pp. 8–9).[6] He also made a strict distinction between 'science' and 'metaphysics', most succinctly in his laudatory comment on Marx as a sociologist, that 'nowhere did he betray positive science to metaphysics' (1942, p. 10); and between 'science' and 'ideology'. In his discussion of the latter in his *History* (1954, pp. 34–47) Schumpeter recognized that in the social sciences there is indeed 'a wide gate for ideology to enter into this process [of the construction of scientific models]' (p. 42), but argued that the rules of scientific practice 'tend to crush out ideologically conditioned error from the visions from which we start' (p. 43); though in notes intended for the continuation of this introductory part of the book (which was left incomplete) he conceded that 'we have had to make large concessions' to the view that the history of scientific economics is 'a history of ideologies' (p. 44). The intention to distinguish clearly between science and ideology is, however, plain. Finally, Schumpeter asserted, though with more qualifications in his later writings (e.g. in the *History*), the 'unity of science', that is to say, the view that the acquisition of valid knowledge proceeds by essentially the same methods in all spheres of experience – in the social sciences and in the natural sciences – a conception later formulated in Marxist terms, and more intransigently, by Otto Neurath (1931, p. 349) in his exposition of a 'strictly scientific unmetaphysical physicalist sociology'. Schumpeter, for his part, in his article (1906) on mathematical methods in economics, pointed repeatedly to the similarities with their use in the natural sciences as part of his advocacy of their further development in his own discipline; and in *Das Wesen* he emphasized some of the general features of this 'unity of science'.

Equally obviously, Schumpeter was an empiricist, whose conception of economics as an 'exact' science was based in large measure on the view that it deals with 'facts verifiable by observation' (though, in contradistinction to some natural sciences, not by experiment). This view is strongly asserted in *Das Wesen*, and is illustrated particularly by his rejection of the need for any analysis of the individual psyche (such as was implicit in Menger's attempt to establish a foundation for his 'exact' laws) in the study of economic behaviour, which could be simply and directly 'observed' (p. 65). But he was not a radical empiricist, since he also emphasized the need for theory, conceived (in neo-Kantian fashion) as the construction of 'schemas' or 'models' (p. 42) in terms of which more general 'laws' of economic behaviour could be expressed: 'The explanation which our theory achieves is a description of functional relations between the elements of our system, expressed in formulas that are as concise and universal as possible. These formulas we call "laws" ' (p. 43). Schumpeter did not, however, examine the problems raised by these notions of 'model', 'functional relation', and 'law' from the standpoint of a systematically developed, or stated, philosophy of science;[7] and indeed we may say that despite his own claims to the contrary there is very little epistemology or philosophy of science in his writings, but mainly a series of semi-popular reflections on methodology in a narrower sense. Thus, in *Das Wesen* (p. xv) a short paragraph on the opposition between deductive and inductive methods (which figured largely in the *Methodenstreit*) consists merely of some trite remarks to the effect that both have played a part in the generation of propositions. Nevertheless, his rejection of an exclusively empiricist, inductivist method is clear in most of his writings, and is perhaps most sharply expressed in his review (1914a) of Simiand's *La méthode positive en science économique* (1912), which he first criticized severely for its exclusion of formal theory and deductive reasoning from 'positive' economics, and then proceeded to contrast with his own conception of the production of knowledge by theoretical analysis, which had then to be tested, however, by the 'observation of facts' (p. 550). The view Schumpeter expounded here has some resemblance to what was later called the 'hypothetico-deductive' method, except that he spoke of 'verification' rather than 'falsification' and in general expressed great confidence in the possibility of confirming knowledge claims by the direct observation of 'facts'.

The nature of formal theory itself, as I have indicated, was not rigorously analysed by Schumpeter, and there is nothing in his methodological writings that is comparable with the studies made by Menger or by Max Adler. The former (see above, page 7) aimed to establish, as the core of theoretical economics, 'exact types' or concepts and universal 'exact' laws, justified by some (introspectively known) properties of the human mind, among them the 'rule of cognition' (see Milford, pp. 231-4, in Caldwell 1990; but note also the astonishingly diverse interpretations of Menger's philosophy of science revealed by other contributions to this volume). In this attempt there was, I suggest, an important neo-Kantian element, and this was more explicitly stated in the work of Max Adler, who set out to answer, from a Marxist standpoint, the Kantian question, 'how is society possible?' (as an object of human knowledge),[8] and argued that Marx had been able to construct his theory of society by introducing the fundamental concept of 'socialized humanity' (or 'social association'), which Adler (1925) posited as being 'transcendentally given as a category of knowledge'. This concept, he claimed, made possible for the first time an investigation of the causal regularities in social life and a *rapprochement* between the natural sciences and social sciences which would eventually allow them to be brought together in a single scientific conceptual scheme. Adler's philosophical writings from 1904 onwards provided the epistemological foundations of Austro-Marxism as a science of society, and it was from this standpoint that Hilferding, in his critique of Böhm-Bawerk, opposed an economic theory which began with an analysis of the social relations of production to one which started from the subjective valuations of individuals. Here, two alternative 'rational models' confronted each other, one of which Schumpeter entirely ignored, though as I shall show, his later work made increasing, more or less tacit, use of the Austro-Marxist model.

There was implicit in Hilferding's response to Böhm-Bawerk a particular criticism of the kind of empiricist approach adopted by some members of the Austrian school; one which had already been briefly formulated by Marx, and has been elaborated in more recent structuralist and realist philosophies of science. In criticizing 'vulgar economics' Marx (*Capital*, vol. I, pt. III, ch. 2) observed that it 'everywhere sticks to appearances in opposition to the law which regulates and explains them', whereas 'scientific truth is always paradox, if judged by everyday experience, which catches only the delusive appearance of things' (*Value, Price and Profit*, pt. VI). In the same terms, a Marxist structuralist (Godelier 1977, pp. 44-5), in his criticism of functionalism, argued that a scientific analysis is only possible when real structures are taken into account, remembering not to confuse, as empiricism does, the real with the visible . . . structures are not directly visible or observable realities, but levels of reality which exist beyond man's visible relations and whose functioning constitutes the deeper logic of a social system – the underlying order by which the apparent order must be explained.

Similarly, in the realist philosophy of science, and especially in those versions which see Marx as being methodologically committed to scientific realism, empiricism is rejected insofar as it deals with a world of unconnected appearances, ignores the role of theory, and does not conceive laws as stating the tendencies of structures (Bhaskar 1991). Schumpeter, of course, did not neglect theory, but he conceived its role as being to present in a systematic way the given empirical data, not to reorganize them critically with reference to a deeper level of economic life. What is most interesting, however, is that in his later work he was in fact more and more concerned with the analysis of structures (though without formally revising his methodology), and it was in this respect particularly that his thought converged with Marxism.

At this stage, Schumpeter's methodology as it was set out in *Das Wesen* and other writings of that period can be summarized in the following way. It was positivist and empiricist in the senses that I have outlined. It embodied a commitment to 'methodological individualism' which was not, however, grounded in any serious epistemological analysis but was justified merely by saying that it produced 'useable results' (in a narrowly defined field), while a 'social' or collectivist methodology offered 'no intrinsic advantages', and was in any case 'superfluous' in the realm of 'pure theory' (*Das Wesen*, p. 95).[9] It recognized and even emphasized the role of theory in economics as a science, but was not at all clear about the nature of that role: whether it consisted only in a systematization of observed 'facts', or involved also a rational construction of models which imposed a specific order upon the empirical data; and whether it established functional relations or causal connections between the elements of the system it depicted. Finally, this methodology expressed initially a conception of the advancement of science as a process of slow accretion, and either ignored, or treated as alternative but not mutually exclusive 'techniques', such confrontations between rival theoretical schemes as might result in a major paradigm change.

But as I shall argue in the following chapters, Schumpeter himself became the originator, in his subsequent writings, of just such a paradigm change, and in the course of accomplishing this he also modified his methodological stance, although plenty of uncertainties, obscurities, and even contradictions persisted in it. His methodology is, however, only one aspect, and for the most part a subordinate one, of the present study, in which my main purpose is to expound and evaluate his analysis of the nature and development of modern capitalism, and to consider the contribution that this may make to the elaboration of a new economic sociology. In *Das Wesen* Schumpeter declared that the study of method could not be separated from the study of concrete problems, and that 'not the first, but the last chapter of a system should deal with its methodology' (p. xv), though the book itself may seem to contradict this prescription. At all events, in the present study Schumpeter's eventual methodology and philosophy of science will be considered in the light of his analyses of 'concrete problems', and contrasted in some respects with his early *profession de foi*, not least with regard to the relative importance of 'static' and 'dynamic' analysis, and to 'methodological individualism'.

Notes

1. For a short account of the controversy see Fusfeld (1987), and for a more extensive discussion Ritzel (1951). Schumpeter himself commented briefly on the *Methodenstreit*, in *Das Wesen*, and again much later in his discussion of the 'historical school' in economics (1954, pp. 814–15). The most interesting feature of his comments is the preference he expressed on both occasions for some kind of methodological 'pluralism' or 'tolerance' which, as we shall see, was never formulated in a systematic and convincing way.
2. The breadth of Schumpeter's knowledge of the economic literature at an early stage in his career, is shown by his monograph (1914b) on the history of economic doctrines and methods.
3. Schumpeter usually employed the term 'exact', derived from Menger's distinction between 'exact' and 'empirical' laws, to characterize this science.

4. This is intended only as a very brief and incomplete statement of the views on 'scientific revolutions' and 'paradigm changes' expounded in particular by Karl Popper (1934, 1963) and Thomas Kuhn (1962). See also the discussion by the contributors to Lakatos and Musgrave (1970).
5. In a footnote to his discussion Schumpeter declared that 'the word "positive" as used in this connection has nothing whatever to do with philosophical positivism' (1954, p. 8, n. 4), but this refers primarily, I think, to the broader socio-political doctrines of the positivist movement, and it may also reflect his own imperfect knowledge of the positivist philosophy of science.
6. This idea of the progress of science as 'slow accretion' contrasts strongly with more recent conceptions of 'scientific revolutions' (see my n. 4 above), and also, as we shall see, with some of Schumpeter's other ideas, for example about 'gales of creative destruction' (not necessarily confined to the economic sphere).
7. Thus, in *Das Wesen*, Schumpeter diverged from the widely held positivist view that the connection between phenomena, or facts, is one of cause and effect (see, for example, J. S. Mill, 1865, pp. 6-8). His 'laws' were presented as describing 'functional relations', and he expressly disclaimed any intention of discovering 'great causal connections' (p. 44); but in later writings, from 1911 onwards, he regularly used the concept of causation (even declaring, in *Business Cycles*, p. 34, that 'the question of causation is the Fundamental Question'), without accounting for this change in his methodological stance which made him more of a positivist and brought him closer, in yet another way, to Austro-Marxism.
8. The same question was examined by Simmel (1908) from a different perspective, and Adler (1919), in a short study of Simmel, considered some of the affinities between their two approaches.
9. Schumpeter's whole discussion here was quite remarkably casual and superficial, and in his own subsequent studies he frequently disregarded the method he had outlined. In its later forms methodological individualism was expounded in a more thorough and sophisticated way by Agassi (1966), and in recent times it has become an important component of 'rational choice' analysis. This influential modern approach to economic and social theory has been critically assessed by Hindess (1988), whose criticisms can well be applied to earlier formulations of the method.

CHAPTER 3

THE THEORY OF ECONOMIC DEVELOPMENT

With his book on economic development (1911)[1] Schumpeter embarked on an entirely new course, outlining a different approach to the phenomena of economic life and introducing the themes which gave a distinctive character to all his later work. In his preface to the English edition (1934) he remarked that 'some of the ideas submitted in this book go back as far as 1907; all of them had been worked out by 1909, when the general framework of this analysis of the purely economic features of capitalistic society took the shape which has remained substantially unaltered ever since' (1934, p. ix). These dates are significant. Schumpeter was beginning to construct his new framework at the very time that he was writing *Das Wesen*, which can be considered in retrospect therefore as a valedictory assessment of Austrian marginal utility theory in its application to 'static' equilibrium analysis, although he continued to refer to this kind of analysis in some of his later writings; for the most part inappropriately and unnecessarily, as I shall show. What is also important is that in 1907 the confrontation between the Austro-Marxist and the Austrian conceptions of economic theory, in Böhm-Bawerk's seminar, was still fresh in Schumpeter's mind, and its influence on his change of direction seems to me unmistakable. Indeed, he recognized it very clearly himself, in the second chapter of *Economic Development*, where he distinguished between the prevalent accounts of economic development or 'progress' which related it to changes in social circumstances or the 'social framework', and an account which would deal with changes *immanent* in the economy, and more specifically changes in technique and in productive organization, which

> require special analysis and evoke something different again from disturbances in the theoretical sense. The non-recognition of this is the most important single reason for what appears unsatisfactory to us in economic theory. From this insignificant-looking source flows, as we shall see, a new conception of the economic process, which overcomes a series of fundamental difficulties and thus justifies the new statement of the problem in the text. This statement of the problem is more nearly parallel to that of Marx. For according to him there is an *internal* economic development and no mere adaptation of economic life to changing data. (footnote, p. 60)[2]

This affinity with Marx is stated again, and more strongly, in the preface to the Japanese edition of *Economic Development* (1937) where Schumpeter wrote:

> it was not clear to me at the outset what to the reader will perhaps be obvious at once, namely, that this idea and this aim [to construct 'a purely economic theory of economic change'] are exactly the same as the idea and the aim which underlie the economic teaching of Karl Marx. In fact, what distinguishes him from the economists of his own time and those who preceded him, was precisely a vision of economic evolution as a distinct process generated by the economic system itself.

In the first chapter of *Economic Development* Schumpeter expounded the principles of a 'static' analysis of the 'circular flow of economic life', based upon marginal utility theory and equilibrium analysis, making frequent references to his previous work, *Das Wesen*. It is important to note here that he did not identify a static analysis with the analysis of a 'stationary economy', but argued that a static analysis may also be applied to an economy which is changing as a result of external influences.[3] In effect, he contrasted two different economic theories, one of which focuses on the analysis of the 'circular flow' and such disturbances as are induced by changes in external data (population changes, social influences and so on), the other on disruption and development produced by changes within the economic system itself. The latter theory he then treated as corresponding more closely with the real evolution of the modern capitalist economy:

> It is just this occurrence of the 'revolutionary' change that is our problem, the problem of economic development in a very narrow and formal sense. The reason why we so state the problem and turn aside from traditional theory lies not so much in the fact that economic changes, especially, if not solely, in the capitalist epoch, have actually occurred thus and not by continuous adaptation, but more in their fruitfulness. (p. 63)

Notwithstanding the different emphasis, this passage is strikingly reminiscent of the characterization of modern capitalism by Marx and Engels in the *Communist Manifesto* (section I): 'Constant revolutionising of production, uninterrupted disturbance of all social conditions, everlasting uncertainty and agitation distinguish the bourgeois epoch from all earlier ones', though its scope is narrower (see n. 2). Even Schumpeter's emphasis on the 'fruitfulness' of his theory, as against its correspondence with the reality of capitalist development, cites among the problems in which its 'fruitfulness' will be demonstrated several – capital, credit, entrepreneurial profit, and crises (or business cycles) – to which Marxist thinkers, and notably Hilferding (1910), had already given particular attention.

That Schumpeter was here setting out an alternative economic theory is made clearer by some of his later comments. In his preface to the English edition (1934, p. ix) he wrote that while he did not wish to maintain that the book was 'satisfactory in every detail', he did 'consider both the outlines – what might be termed the "vision" – and the results as correct in the main'. This idea of a 'vision' is expressed more fully in an essay on Keynes (1946a):

> Every comprehensive 'theory' of an economic state of society consists of two complementary but essentially distinct elements. There is, first, the theorist's view about the basic features of that state of society, about what is and what is not important in order to understand its life at a given time. Let us call this his vision. And there is, second, the theorist's technique, an apparatus by which he conceptualizes his vision and which turns the latter into concrete propositions or 'theories'.

And as I noted earlier (above page 22), Schumpeter used the notion of 'vision' again in his *History*, in discussing the relation between economic science and ideology.

This combination of 'vision' and 'technique' we can, I think, legitimately refer to as a 'paradigm', in some important senses of that term – as a 'philosophy' or constellation of questions, an organizing principle, and the source of conceptual and instrumental tools (see Masterman 1970) – and then say that in *Economic Development* Schumpeter introduced a new paradigm which he contrasted sharply with that of the Austrian school and likened in important respects to that of Marx. Whether at this stage he thought that the 'traditional' Austrian theory could be criticized from this new standpoint, or was transcended by it, or whether these were two incommensurable paradigms both of which made an important contribution to our understanding of different aspects of economic life, is not altogether clear.[4] Certainly, after expounding the Austrian theory in the first chapter of the book, he went on to express his dissatisfaction with its limitations, and in a later article on Menger (1921) he observed that 'no economic sociology or sociology of economic development can be derived from Menger's work. It makes only a small contribution to the picture of economic history and the struggle of social classes'; but he then added that 'Menger's theory of value, price, and distribution is the best we have up to now' (p. 86).

The substance of Schumpeter's book, however, had little to do with Austrian value theory or with equilibrium analysis. Its originality lay in its concentration on an analysis, and at least potentially an explanation, of the process of development of the capitalist economy, along lines 'parallel to Marx'. Schumpeter formulated his new approach by saying that economic life experiences changes 'which do not appear continously and which change the framework, the traditional course itself. They cannot be understood by means of any analysis of the circular flow, although they are purely economic and although their explanation is obviously among the tasks of pure theory' (p. 61). The question to be answered is then 'how do such changes take place, and to what economic phenomena do they give rise?' (p. 62), and Schumpeter stated his basis proposition by saying that such spontaneous and discontinuous changes – 'development' in his sense – are defined 'by the carrying out of new combinations' (which covers the introduction of a new goal or a new method of production, the opening of a new market, the conquest of a new source of supply of raw materials or semi-manufactured goods, or the carrying out of the new organization of any industry) (p. 66).

From this starting-point he continued his argument by observing that the carrying out of new combinations required command over means of production, and that this was made possible by the provision of credit, 'the characteristic method of the capitalist type of society'.[5] Finally, he added to these two elements of his analysis – 'new combinations of means of production', and 'credit' – a third, which 'may be described as the fundamental phenomenon of economic development. The carrying out of new combinations we call "enterprise"; the individuals whose function it is to carry them out we call "entrepreneurs" ' (p. 74).

With the specification of these three elements Schumpeter's model of economic development was virtually complete, and much of the rest of his book was devoted to a more detailed study of some related phenomena – the nature and function of credit, entrepreneurial profit, and interest on capital. In the concluding chapter (Chapter 6, as revised in the 1926 edition), however, Schumpeter embarked on an enquiry into a major feature of capitalist development, namely, economic crises, or 'recurrent business fluctuations', which was pursued on a much larger scale in his book of 1939, and introduced some of his most distinctive ideas about the functioning of a capitalist economy. His initial discussion is of great interest both methodologically and in its substantive analysis. In the first place he now claimed to establish causal connections: 'I explain the phenomenon of business fluctuations . . . solely by an objective chain of causation which runs its course automatically'; and he described this causal process as 'the effect of the appearance of new enterprises upon the conditions of the existing ones' (p. 213). Responding to criticisms of the first edition that he did not try to explain why entrepreneurs should 'appear periodically in swarms', he argued that in the chapter outlining his general theory of economic development (Chapter 2) he had in fact provided an explanation (whether or not it was conclusive) in terms of the appearance of new advantageous possibilities for entrepreneurs. He went on to compare his theory with that of Spiethoff (deriving from Juglar), agreeing with him on many points; e.g. that 'the wave-like fluctuations in business and not the crisis itself appears to be the fundamental thing to be explained', and 'alternating situations are the form economic development takes in the era of capitalism' (pp. 214–15). He also agreed that 'the causal nexus begins first of all with the means of production', and 'the circumstance which cuts short the boom' is the overproduction of capital goods, but he saw as the distinctive feature of his own theory the emphasis on the emergence of new enterprises *en masse*, the effect of which is 'so to change all the conditions that a special process of adaptation becomes necessary' (p. 216).

But this periodic 'swarming' of entrepreneurs was not yet fully explained, and Schumpeter in fact went on to refer to some objections, such as whether crises are 'a uniform phenomenon', and whether they are 'capable of a purely economic explanation', which tend to weaken his theory. He concluded, however, that 'there is, at all events, one class of crises, which are *elements*, or at any rate regular if not necessary *incidents*, of a wave-like motion of alternating periods of prosperity and depression, which have pervaded economic life ever since the capitalist era began' (p. 223),[6] and offered as his explanation of this wave-like motion, resulting from the appearance of entrepreneurs, not continuously, but in clusters, simply that 'the appearance of one or two entrepreneurs facilitates the appearance of others, and these the appearance of more, in ever-increasing numbers' (p. 228). He went on to say that 'every normal boom starts in one or a few branches of industry (railway building, electrical, and chemical industries, and so forth)', and 'derives its character from the innovations in the industry where it begins' (p. 229). The 'pioneers' or 'innovators' remove obstacles not only in their own branch of production but also in others, and so the swarm of entrepreneurs grows. But the boom is necessarily followed by a depression: it 'creates out of itself an *objective situation*, which . . . leads *easily* to a crisis, *necessarily* to a depression' (p. 236), and the various phases of the economic cycle 'now appear as parts of a single causal nexus' (p. 237).

The theory of capitalist development which Schumpeter presented here, in a very original form, and in strictly causal terms, was elaborated in later essays, and above all in his massive study of business cycles, with reference to which I shall examine (in Chapter 5) the subsequent criticisms of his theory, as well as comparing it with other theories of economic crises. But *Economic Development* also contains observations which point towards different aspects of Schumpeter's later work. Thus, the idea of the 'vanishing entrepreneur', which occupies an important place in his analysis of the decline of capitalism (1942) is already briefly stated:

> The more accurately . . . we learn to know the natural and social worlds, the more perfect our control of facts becomes; and the greater the extent, with time and progressive rationalisation, within which things can be simply calculated, and indeed quickly and reliably calculated, the more the significance of this function [of entrepreneurship and economic leadership] decreases. Therefore the importance of the entrepreneur type must diminish. (pp. 85–6)

And at the end of the book he considered various economic policies which might moderate the economic fluctuations, while leading into 'a special variety of economic planning' (p. 254), but concluded nevertheless that 'in a society with private property and competition' there is no therapy that 'can permanently obstruct the great economic and social process by which businesses, individual positions, forms of life, cultural values and ideals, sink in the social scale and finally disappear' (p. 255). These reflections, along with others scattered throughout the book, reveal the increasingly sociological and historical orientation of Schumpeter's thought, and they clearly anticipate major themes in much of his later writing; for example, in the monograph on social classes (1927b) and in the analysis of the social system and changing civilization of capitalism (1942).

Between 1911 and the publication of his next major work in 1939, Schumpeter wrote, for the series *Grundriss der Sozialökonomik*, a short study (1914b) of the history of economic doctrines and methods, which included a relatively substantial discussion of Marx's economics (later expanded in Schumpeter 1942) but strangely ignored later Marxist thinkers, and notably Hilferding, who had replied to the critics of Marx's theory; and he also published a great number of articles and monographs in diverse areas of economic theory, economic policy, and sociology. During this time he had a varied career, as professor of economics at the University of Graz from 1911 to 1921, with an intermission as visiting professor at Columbia University in 1913–14, and a further absence in 1919 when he acted, for a few months, as a consultant to the Socialization Commission in Berlin (of which Hilferding was a member) and was then, for a short period (March–October 1919), Secretary of the Treasury (finance minister) in the coalition government of the first Austrian Republic, sponsored by the socialist party (SPÖ) and more particularly, it seems, by Otto Bauer. In 1921 he applied for further leave of

The theory of economic development 35

absence from the university and finally submitted his resignation, having accepted the presidency of a private bank in Vienna. There he remained until 1925, when he became professor of economics at the University of Bonn (with visiting appointments at Harvard University in 1927–8 and 1930), and finally moved to Harvard as professor of economics in 1932.

Among the most important of Schumpeter's writings in these decades are the monographs on imperialism (1919) and social classes (1927b), which will be discussed in the next chapter, a short study of the 'tax state' (1918), his first article on socialism (1920/21), an essay on the instability of capitalism (1928b), several articles on the entrepreneur, and especially in the 1930s numerous articles on business cycles. In addition, Schumpeter wrote frequently on current economic problems and policies, and on the methods of the social sciences, more particularly economics, in articles, book reviews and obituary or biographical notices (some of the latter being collected in Schumpeter 1952). From these writings we can gain a clearer idea of the changes in Schumpeter's intellectual orientation – in his 'vision' or 'paradigm' – and the development of his own distinctive views, already adumbrated in *Economic Development*, which led to the later major studies of business cycles and of capitalism and socialism. The first point to note is that he effectively – if not always quite unambiguously – abandoned the approach of the Austrian school in three important respects: (i) by focusing his analysis on the capitalist economy rather than on an abstractly conceived 'economy' as such; (ii) by concentrating increasingly on capitalist *production* instead of on *exchange* (which in his first book, *Das Wesen*, he had declared to be the central problem for economic theory); and (iii) by emphasizing the dynamic nature of capitalism, and hence the methodological imperative to analyse the *process* of capitalist production from a historical and sociological perspective.

In all these respects Shumpeter drew closer to Marxist economic theory, as he recognized on several occasions, and his writings from 1911 onwards are distinguished, among other features, especially by the fact that unlike almost all other academic economists of his time he gave serious, if incomplete, consideration to Marxist economics and social theory, as well as to the possibility that a socialist economy might follow capitalism. His mature critique of Marxism and his own analysis of the 'decline of capitalism' (1942) will be examined in Chapter 6, but there are two essays of the 1920s which already present some elements of his later argument. In the first of these (Schumpeter 1920/21) he considered the prospects for socialism in Europe – and more specifically in Austria and Germany – at a time when he, like his teacher Wieser, was sympathetically inclined towards the socialist movement. He had taken part in the work of the German Commission on Socialization and had served as finance minister in the Austrian government of 1919, where the SPÖ, as the largest party in the constituent assembly, played a major part and had as one of its principal domestic objectives the 'planned and systematic socialization of all the branches of national economy' which were 'ripe for this purpose'. Otto Bauer outlined a plan for socialization in a series of articles in the *Arbeiter Zeitung* (January 1919, reprinted as a booklet, Bauer 1919), and in March 1919 a socialization commission was established, which elected Bauer as president (Gulick 1948, vol. I, pp. 135–7).[7] Schumpeter, who was closely involved in the discussions about socialization, and during his time as finance minister with governmental decisions,[8] wrote in his article of 1920/21 that 'everyone talks about socialization', and that the 'present inner meaning of a revolution, [its] sustaining idea . . . can only be socialization'. He proposed, therefore, to analyse its meaning, its practical significance, and its possibilities in the existing situation in Germany and Austria.

Schumpeter began by observing that 'socialization' had become a popular slogan among the most diverse groups of people, and that socialists themselves differed about the methods and the goal of the process, so that the term had lost all precision. Furthermore, the literature on the subject was marked, in his opinion, by an extreme banality and a failure to deal seriously with fundamental issues and problems.[9] He therefore set out, very precisely, his own conception:

> Here I want to discuss only real socialization, i.e. socialization in the sense of the transformation of an economy based upon private property and private initiative into a socialist economy . . . in which a central body disposes of all means of production [and] elaborates and carries out an economic plan for society . . . Socialization could therefore signify both a gradual historical process, and conscious political action directed towards this end. Such political action can only lead to results, however, if a historical, automatic socialization

process, inscribed in the nature of things, has already started, and social development itself contributes to socialism. This perception we owe above all to Karl Marx. It distinguishes scientific socialism from utopian socialism . . . which expresses nothing but the longing of the human heart for paradise. (pp. 458–9)

He continued his exposition by arguing that there was undoubtedly a tendency towards socialization, revealed by the increasing dominance of large enterprises, the concentration of capital in industry and finance, and the formation of trusts, as Marx had indicated (and as Hilferding had shown more fully in *Finance Capital* (1910), which Schumpeter does not mention although it evidently provided much of the background for his own ideas). In the modern capitalist economy, large bureaucratic organizations have a dominant position, and a process of rationalization goes on continuously, bringing socialism closer as it strengthens the possibility of substituting a conscious and deliberate rationalization for an automatic and unregulated one. Schumpeter's discussion of this process (pp. 464–8) is close to the conceptions of Max Weber, not only in the issues it raises but also in its general sociological approach, and was most probably influenced by Weber's writings (though here too, as in the case of Hilferding, there is no reference to an important source of Schumpeter's own views).[10]

One of the most distinctive aspects of his analysis, however – anticipating much of his later work – concerns the changing role of the entrepreneur. At first, he observed, the entrepreneurial innovator played an important role in the restructuring of the economy; but an ever larger part of the entrepreneurial function, and of business leadership, has come to consist in the application of principles which can be demonstrated and learned. Economic progress becomes increasingly 'impersonal', and eventually, in some distant future, the economy will be 'a single great machine, developing automatically' through 'systematically organized office work' rather than the actions of 'leading personalities' (p. 468).

After expounding in this way his conception of the socialization process, Schumpeter examined some of its political concomitants in a transition to socialism, and the methods by which this culminating stage of socialization might be attained. The establishment of a socialist economy, he thought, would necessarily be accompanied by changes in the political system, broadly characterized as a movement from an exclusively parliamentary democracy (in his view a creation of the bourgeoisie) to a 'council' democracy, in which factory councils or workers' councils would play a major political role and would bring into existence new institutions.[11] In considering the methods by which full socialization (i.e. socialism) could be achieved, Schumpeter made some important points about the pre-conditions for any effective action towards this end: first, as he had noted earlier, 'a wealth of existing capital' (p. 472), and then 'the emergence of giant enterprises in which the rationalization of production had established itself, and machines and calculation began to transform the human psyche' (pp. 481–2). The technical 'possibility' of socialization in this sense already existed in some capitalist countries, but the time when action could be confidently undertaken to bring about a transition still lay far in the future (p. 482), as was shown, he considered, by the political weakness of the movements towards socialism throughout Europe. This phenomenon raised questions about the viability of attempts at 'premature' socialization, and more generally about the manner in which it should be undertaken; whether 'full' socialization would be essential from the outset, or whether the goal might be reached more effectively through a process of successive 'partial' socializations (pp. 483–90).[12] Schumpeter emphasized particularly the disruption and economic hardship that 'full' socialization would cause, but noted two methods by which it might be implemented with less dire consequences (through what may be regarded as a policy situated somewhere between 'full' and 'partial' socialization) in the conditions of post-war capitalism: first, by socializing the major banks and thus establishing control over a large part of industry, as Hilferding had already suggested in *Finance Capital* (1910); and secondly, by forming compulsory associations, regulated by the state, in the principal sectors of industry, as had been done during the period of the 'war economy' (pp. 492–3).

Nevertheless, Schumpeter reached the conclusion that any kind of socialization in the socialist sense would have generally harmful consequences in the immediate post-war circumstances, and that for social as well as economic reasons its advent in the European countries was unlikely (in Austria impossible, pp. 503–8). 'Nowhere', he wrote, 'is private initiative, the method of the capitalist economy, so indispensable as during and after such a débâcle as we have experienced', and he continued, 'it would have been quite un-Marxist, quite contrary to Marx's scholarly analysis, to expect that the social revolution would spread from Russia to the whole of Europe' (p. 498). But by the time he wrote *Capitalism, Socialism and Democracy* (1942) Schumpeter had quite clearly changed his mind about the prospects for socialism, and one important factor in producing this change was the different assessment he began to make of the stablility of capitalism, initially in his essay of 1928b. Here he proposed to deal with the question 'whether or not the capitalistic system is stable in itself – that is to say, whether or not it would, in the absence of [external, non-economic] disturbances, show any tendency towards self-destruction from inherent economic causes, or towards outgrowing its own frame' (1928b, p. 48). He then defined capitalism as 'an economic system characterized by private property (private initiative), by production for a market and by the phenomenon of credit' and while rejecting the idea that economic history can be 'divided into epochs corresponding to different systems' nevertheless argued that

> it is still permissible to date the *prevalence* of capitalistic methods from about the middle of the eighteenth century (for England), and to call the nineteenth century . . . the time of *competitive*, and what has so far followed, the time of increasingly 'trustified', or otherwise 'organised', 'regulated' or 'managed' capitalism. (p. 48)

For important elements in this definition Schumpeter was heavily indebted to the work of Hilferding, who had already emphasized (1910) the importance of credit creation by the banks and the rapid growth of trusts and cartels in the 'latest phase of capitalist development', and had introduced (in articles of the early 1920s) the terms 'organized capitalism' and the 'organized economy' to describe the post-war changes. Schumpeter then, additionally, made a distinction between two senses of 'stability': one in which it refers to the question of the institutional survival of capitalism (i.e. of the capitalist *order*); the other referring to the stability or instability of business conditions' (i.e. the business cycle). But 'of course, mere instability of the "system" would if severe enough, threaten the stability of the "order" or the "system" may have an inherent tendency to destroy the "order" by undermining the social positions on which the "order" rests' (p. 49).

Following this delineation of his subject matter Schumpeter

proposed to translate 'the business man's meaning of stability . . . into the language of theory' and proceeded to sketch the principles of static, equilibrium analysis along the familiar lines of (mainly) Austrian theory. But all this, he then showed, was quite irrelevant to his main argument. The 'received doctrine', that 'industrial expansion, automatically incident to, and moulded by, general social growth – of which the most important purely economic forces are growth of population and of savings – is the basic fact about economic change or evolution or "progress" ' (p. 61), is 'inadequate, or even misleading' as a description of the mechanism of economic life, for 'expansion is *no* basic fact, capable of serving in the role of a cause, but is itself the result of a more fundamental "economic force" ' (p. 62), namely 'innovation', which is the function of entrepreneurs (or economic leaders) as he had argued in *Economic Development*. The process is 'essentially discontinuous' and 'does not lend itself to description in terms of a theory of equilibrium' (p. 64). This theory, one might suppose, should therefore be explicitly discarded, but Schumpeter never proceeded quite so far, although in most of his later writings he largely ignored it or made only brief, and in my estimation ritual, acknowledgements to it. In this essay, at all events, after summing up his view that

> there is, indeed, one element in the capitalist process, embodied in the type and function of the entrepreneur, which will . . . destroy any equilibrium that may have established itself or been in process of being established . . . [and] produces the cyclical 'waves' which are essentially the form 'progress' takes in competitive capitalism

he goes on to say that in 'periods of depression a new equilibrium always emerges, or tends to emerge, which absorbs the results of innovation carried out in the preceding periods of prosperity' (p. 69).

Schumpeter concluded his article with two observations which are important for the later development of his ideas. First, he noted the effects of the change from 'competitive' to 'organized' capitalism; in the latter, 'innovation is not any more embodied *typically* in new firms, but goes on, within the big units now existing, largely independently of individual persons' (p. 70), and this diminishes the role of the individual entrepreneur, and more generally brings changes in 'motives, stimuli and styles of life'

(p. 71). But it may also be that 'the only fundamental cause of instability inherent to the capitalist system is losing in importance as time goes on, and may even be expected to disappear' (p. 71).[13] Secondly, however, he considered that capitalism

> creates, by rationalising the human mind, a mentality and a style of life incompatible with its own fundamental conditions, motives and social institutions, and will be changed, although not by economic necessity and probably even at some sacrifice of economic welfare, into an order of things which will be merely a matter of taste and terminology to call Socialism or not. (p. 72)

Between 1911 and the late 1920s Schumpeter elaborated further his entirely new 'vision' of the economic process, in which three major elements stand out prominently. First, as I noted earlier (above, page 35), he defined as the central problem for economic analysis the development of capitalism as a system of *production*, and outlined a theory to explain that development. This clearly separated him from the kind of analysis which focused on economic behaviour in general and on *exchange* relationships. Secondly, he distinguished two main phases in capitalist development: the 'competitive' and the 'organized' (alternatively described as 'trustified', 'regulated' or 'managed'); and his analysis of the second phase led him to consider the possibility that a socialist economy would follow capitalism. Thirdly, his preoccupation with economic development necessarily involved a historical approach to economic analysis, and more fundamentally, a conception of economic systems as historical realities which come into existence under particular conditions, evolve and then in other conditions are, or may be, transformed into a new and different system. At the same time, this historical vision became increasingly sociological, taking account of the social framework which sustained, or might change, a particular economic system, and of the effects of economic development on the social framework itself. For this outlook Schumpeter was no doubt partly indebted to Wieser,[14] and to Max Weber and Pareto, but above all to the Marxist 'economic interpretation of history'; and his own broad scheme of thought can itself be regarded, with qualifications, as a form of 'economic interpretation', being in that sense thoroughly sociological. It is evident, in any case, that a sociological approach becomes increasingly prominent in his work – tentatively suggested in *Economic Development*, employed in his study of the 'tax-state' (1918), and in the distinction made in his article (1928b) between the instability of capitalism as an economic 'system' and its instability as a social 'order', but most clearly articulated, in this period, in his monographs on imperialism (1919) and on social classes (1927b).[15] It is with these two studies that I shall begin, in the next chapter, an exploration of some basic themes in Schumpeter's sociology.

Notes

1. A second edition appeared in 1926, for which Schumpeter rewrote Chapters 2 and 6, omitted Chapter 7, and made other minor revisions. The English version (1934) is based on this second edition, and I have used the English text throughout my discussion, since as Schumpeter said (1934, p. ix), the changes he made in it were only of 'expository consequence' and did not affect the central argument of the book.
2. Schumpeter added, however, that 'my structure covers only a small part of his [Marx's] ground'. The whole of this long footnote, beginning on p. 59, is extremely valuable in making clear the distinctiveness of Schumpeter's new approach.
3. He explained this clearly (p. 82, n. 1) in the following passage: '"Static" theory does not assume a stationary economy; it also treats of the effects of changes in data. In itself, therefore, there is no necessary connection between static theory and stationary reality. Only in so far as one can exhibit the fundamental form of the economic course of events with the maximum simplicity in an unchanging economy does this assumption recommend itself to theory.'
4. Although he suggests the latter view when he says of the Austrian theory and the theory of development that 'the two methods lie in different planes' (p. 61).
5. In later articles (1928b, 1946b) he included credit as a defining characteristic of capitalism: thus 'the institution of bank credit is so essential to the functioning of the capitalist system that, although not strictly implied in the definition, it should be added to the other two criteria [private ownership of means of production, and production by private initiative for private profit]' (1946b, p. 184). It should be remembered, in considering the emphasis on credit in Chapters 2 and 3 of *Economic Development* and in later writings, that Hilferding

The theory of economic development 43

(1910) had already set out the importance of credit creation by the banks in a work with which Schumpeter was undoubtedly familiar, and to which he was in various ways indebted.

6. In a footnote he attributed 'this discovery and the full perception of its consequences' to Clément Juglar, but in the preface to the English edition of *Economic Development* (1934) he declared himself convinced that there were at least three wave-like movements, and this view was fully developed in *Business Cycles* (1939).
7. However, the practical achievements of the socialization programme were limited, and after the collapse of the Hungarian 'Soviet republic' in August 1919, enthusiasm for socialization diminished somewhat even among the SPÖ leaders, who regarded it increasingly as a long-term and gradual process. For a more detailed account, see Gulick (1948, vol. I, ch. 8).
8. His resignation from the government in October 1919 was provoked by a conflict over the proposed socialization of the *Alpine Montan Gesellschaft*. See Gulick (1948, vol. I, pp. 139–40) who cites Schumpeter's subsequent comment on the affair; also Schumpeter's letter to the Austrian Chancellor (Renner) in Schumpeter (1985, pp. 337–43) and the comment by the editors in the same volume (pp. 27–30).
9. This is reminiscent of the comment made by Otto Neurath (1920) on the proceedings of the German Socialization Commission, that because socialists had previously only offered criticism of capitalist society, 'when revolution broke out, a commission for socialization had to be called to discuss the basic principles. Longwinded, sterile debates took place showing disagreements of all sorts, without producing a uniform programme.'
10. Economic rationalization continued to be a major subject of discussion through the 1920s and 1930s, particularly in relation to the development of 'scientific management' (Taylorism) and 'mass production/mass consumption' (Fordism) in the capitalist countries, and on the other side, to economic planning and massive industrialization in the Soviet Union. From the Austro-Marxist standpoint, Otto Bauer (1931) wrote a substantial critical assessment of capitalist rationalization and its limits, and Hilferding, in the 1920s, developed his conception of 'organized capitalism' as a partly rationalized and planned economic system.
11. The idea of 'council democracy', and in a broader and looser sense, 'industrial democracy' or 'economic democracy', was widely discussed among socialists at this time, in the context of the emergence of 'soviets' as a major element in the Russian Revolution and in the revolutionary movements in Germany and Hungary. Schumpeter himself argued (1920/21, p. 474) that 'socialization and the council

system belong together and tend to realize themselves together', but among the Austro-Marxists (and socialists generally) opinion was divided and Karl Renner (1921), for example, in a critical review of the question, noted the limitations of the council system and insisted on the need for both economic and political (parlimentary) democracy.

12. The latter course was the one proposed by Otto Bauer (1919) in his conception of the 'slow revolution', and it was followed, so far as possible, by the SPÖ from 1918 to 1934.
13. This is remarkably close to Hilferding's view that 'organized capitalism' had brought greater stability, largely through the introduction of a degree of economic planning by corporations themselves and by a more interventionist state. See also the interpretation of this period of stability as a 'trial run for corporatism', by Peukert (1991, ch. 5). Schumpeter, however, paid less attention to the economic role of the state, and even in later writings referred to it only briefly, generally in disparaging terms.
14. See his reference (1927a, p. 301) to Wieser's 'historical sociology' or 'sociological history'.
15. Schumpeter, it seems, counted these two studies among his most important scientific writings; see the introduction by Paul Sweezy to Schumpeter (1919, p. vii).

CHAPTER 4

SOCIOLOGICAL EXCURSIONS

Schumpeter's monograph on the 'sociology of imperialisms' was written during the First World War and published in 1919.[1] At that time imperialism, as a new phase in the development of capitalism, was already a major issue for social theorists – above all for Marxist thinkers – and the war itself, as it continued remorselessly with immense loss of life, engendered fierce political controversy, which reached a climax in 1917 after the October Revolution in Russia and the growth of anti-war and revolutionary movements in much of Europe. The analyses of imperialism by Hobson (1902), Hilferding (1910), Luxemburg (1913), Bukharin (1915),[2] and Lenin (1916), formed a background against which Schumpeter pursued his own study, although he was not familiar with all these writings and drew mainly on the work of Hilferding, and to some extent of Otto Bauer, who are referred to in his text as the 'neo-Marxists'. The study, according to Schumpeter himself (p. 8), was a contribution to 'the sociology of the Zeitgeist' ('spirit of the age') insofar as it dealt with the neo-Marxist theory – 'by far the most serious contribution toward a solution of our problem' – and in a footnote he referred to his book on the crisis of the tax state as approaching the same problem 'from another angle', and to a forthcoming work on 'the central ideas of socialism' – subsequently transformed into the article on 'the possibilities of socialism' (1920/21) which I discussed in the previous chapter – that would 'deal with a related complex of ideas'.

Schumpeter began by observing that 'aggressive attitudes on the part of states [or of earlier organizational structures] can be explained, directly and unequivocally, only in part by the real and concrete interests of the people' (p. 3). After a brief discussion of the notion of 'interests' he then offered as a general definition of imperialism: 'the objectless disposition on the part of a state to unlimited expansion' (p. 7) – a curious formulation which will require closer examination. It may be possible, he then suggested, 'in the final analysis, to give an "economic explanation" for this phenomenon', but he proposed first to 'analyze the birth and life of imperialism by means of historical examples', regarded as 'typical'. A 'common basic trait', he claimed, 'emerges in every case ... though there are substantial differences among the individual cases. Hence the plural, "imperialisms" ' (p. 8).

The first case is that of Britain in the later nineteenth century, where Schumpeter considered that imperialism was just a 'catch phrase', impotent in terms of practical politics because of the 'absence of warlike structural elements in the social organization' (p. 29). Imperialism in practice he then examined in the cases of ancient Egypt, Persia, the Assyrians, France in the age of Louis XIV, the Arabs, the Germanic tribes, particularly the Franks, and the Roman Empire. In the course of this hasty survey, he introduced the conception of 'warrior nations': 'the imperialism of a warrior nation, a people's imperialism, appears in history when a people has acquired a warlike disposition and a corresponding social organization, *before* it has had an opportunity to be absorbed in the peaceful exploitation of its definitive area of settlement' (p. 36), but he also noted, with reference to the later history of the Franks, that 'not every warlike nation tends towards imperialism' (p. 60). Next, Schumpeter briefly considered the nature of imperialism in the age of the modern absolute monarchy, in France and Russia, where he considered that belligerence and war policies could be explained by necessities of the social structure and 'the inherited dispositions of the ruling class' (p. 77), 'the urge to action of a ruling class disposed to war' (p. 81).

The importance of inherited structures and dispositions was strongly asserted again in the final section of Schumpeter's study where he examined the connection between capitalism and imperialism. In the first place, 'analysis of the historical evidence has shown the unquestionable fact that "objectless" tendencies toward forcible expansion, without definite, utilitarian limits ... play a very large role in the history of mankind' (p. 83); and 'the explanation lies . . . in the vital needs of situations that moulded peoples and classes into warriors – if they wanted to avoid extinction – and in the fact that psychological dispositions and social structures acquired in the dim past . . . once firmly established tend to maintain themselves' (pp. 83–4), this survival being facilitated by various subsidiary factors, including economic interests. He concluded, therefore, that imperialism is 'atavistic in character', and that 'it is from absolute autocracy that the present age has taken over what imperialist tendencies it displays' (p. 85). The Industrial Revolution and the development of capitalism, however, undermine these traditional habits, by their rationalization of life, and 'a purely capitalist world therefore can offer no fertile soil to imperialist impulses' (pp. 86–90).[3] In particular, 'where free trade prevails *no* class has an interest in forcible expansion as such'.

But the growth of protectionism (as in Germany, for example) changed this situation, since it facilitated the formation of cartels and trusts, and altered the alignment of interests, and Schumpeter noted that it was the 'neo-Marxist doctrine of Bauer and Hilferding which first described this causal connection and recognized its significance (p. 104). In these circumstances military conquest, or what Hilferding defined as the 'struggle for economic territory' by force or the threat of force (which Hitler subsequently justified by the need for *Lebensraum*) acquired great economic importance, and Schumpeter summarized the new state of affairs as one in which

> we have . . . within a social group that carries great political weight, a strong, undeniable, economic interest in such things as protective tariffs, cartels, monopoly prices, forced exports (dumping), an aggressive economic policy, and aggressive foreign policy generally, and war, including wars of expansion with a typically imperialist character . . . [and] once this alignment of interests exists, an even stronger interest in a somewhat differently motivated expansion must be added . . . the conquest of lands producing raw materials and foodstuffs, with a view to facilitating self-sufficient warfare. (p. 110)

Nevertheless, he went on to warn against overestimating 'this aspect of modern economic life' (p. 111), pointing out how export monopolism injured the workers and was 'anything but a brilliant success, even for the entrepreneurs' (p. 115). In the final pages of his book Schumpeter rejected the Marxist view of this latest, inevitable phase of capitalism, arguing that 'export monopolism does *not* grow from the inherent laws of capitalist development' and 'there is no tendency toward combination inherent in the competitive system' (p. 117). Protectionism, in the form of tariffs, is to be traced back to the financial interests of the absolute monarchies, and the life, ideology and politics of the European countries are still 'greatly under this influence of the feudal "substance" ' (p. 122). Both nationalism and militarism are rooted in the autocratic state, and imperialism *fuses* with them (p. 128), but 'in the end the climate of the modern world must destroy' these pre-capitalist elements in social life, and 'imperialisms will wither and die' (pp. 129–30).[4]

The theory that Schumpeter expounded in 1919 is open to numerous objections, and it has been widely criticized, from various standpoints. Aron (1958), in a note on Veblen and Schumpeter at the end of his monograph (see note 4 on page 59 below), suggested that the latter 'seems to have had increasing doubts about explaining imperialism exclusively in terms of survivals of the past' (p. 63). Indeed Schumpeter himself appeared ready to abandon the theory later on, when he wrote (1939, p. 696, n.1) that a 'glimpse of a view that now seems to the writer to be nearer the truth than either the Marxist or his own ['atavism'] theory is embodied in Karl Renner's concept of Social Imperialism (Sozialimperialismus)'. But this brief comment is both misleading and vague. Renner, who was a leading Austro-Marxist, was arguing in the book to which Schumpeter presumably refers (Renner 1917) *against* the views of those who maintained that the working class might gain from an imperialist policy, just as Hilferding (1910, ch. 25) had done earlier (see Sweezy 1951), pp. xvi–xviii), so that it is difficult to see how Schumpeter could reasonably attribute to Renner a conception of 'social imperialism' as the 'imperialism of a whole people' (Winslow 1948, pp. 235–6), if that indeed is what he intended. In any case, Schumpeter had no more to say about what he understood as social imperialism, which may or may not have corresponded with his own idea of 'warrior peoples', who were now re-emerging, for reasons that remain obscure, in the supposedly pacific capitalist societies; and in his only subsequent discussion of the subject (1942, pp. 49–55) he confined himself to repeating earlier criticisms of the neo-Marxist (i.e. principally Austro-Marxist) theory. It should also be noted, however, that in his later writings Schumpeter, having assimilated the Marxist conception of 'socialization', at least in the sense of the growth of large corporations, simply contradicted his original assertion that there is no inherent tendency towards combination in the competitive system (above, page 48).

In the end it is very doubtful whether Schumpeter had a settled theory of imperialism at all, but such elements of a theory as emerge from his early study and his later arguments against Marxism, have faced a great deal of criticism. Thus Lichtheim (1971) claimed that Schumpeter, in his description of imperialism as atavistic,

> juggles with the term 'imperialism'. True, the European middle class had grown up within an absolutist framework, allowed the landed nobility to run the government for it, and even propped up the dynastic empires of the Hohenzollerns, Habsburgs, and Romanovs. But that same middle class had by 1914 spawned a plutocratic upper stratum which coalesced with the ruling elites of the ancient monarchies and rendered them more, rather than less, aggressive and expansionist. (pp. 127–8)

Furthermore, 'Schumpeter undercut his own position by taking over the *laissez-faire* argument and then reluctantly conceding the validity of the Marxist thesis concerning the link between protectionism, monopoly capitalism, and external aggression' (p. 128). Finally, 'on Schumpeter's assumptions, as stated in 1919' – summed up in the view that a 'people's imperialism' is today impossible – 'Italian and German fascism are inexplicable', whereas in fact 'a "people's imperialism" was just what the Italian and German working classes – or anyway the bulk of them – came to believe in for a time' (p. 129). But as we have seen, in 1939 Schumpeter – perhaps mainly influenced by the experience of fascism – had apparently adopted the idea of a 'people's imperialism', though without explaining what he meant by the term; and Lichtheim's own use of this concept is questionable, for it was not the case that 'the bulk' of the working class in Italy, or especially in Germany, supported the nationalistic, militaristic and expansionist aims of the fascist movements, or 'believed in' a people's imperialism, before these movements seized power.[5] In Germany, the major part of the working class, up to the last free election in

November 1932, continued to vote for the main working-class parties – which were opposed to imperialism, the Social Democratic (SPD) and Communist (KPD) parties – while the National Socialist party (NSDAP) never obtained a majority of the total vote.[6]

After his brief comment in 1939, Schumpeter made no further attempt to develop his own theory of imperialism; in *Capitalism, Socialism and Democracy* (1942, pp. 49–55) he largely repeated, and expanded somewhat, his criticisms of the neo-Marxist (Austro-Marxist) theory, and in his *History* (1954) he did not mention the subject at all. But as Amsden (1987, pp. 728–32) has commented, while the neo-classical economists have chosen to ignore such a historically important phenomenon, their 'starting and ending point' being Schumpeter's monograph of 1919, Marxists of various persuasions have continued to make use of the theoretical legacy received from Hilferding, Luxemburg and Lenin (Brewer 1980). One result of their studies has been to show the naiveté of Schumpeter's distinction between the rationality of 'peaceful exchange' and the irrationality of 'forcible expansion' in the circumstances of the twentieth century,[7] for as Amsden notes (*op. cit.*, p. 731), 'at a minimum, force might be rational for one party to hasten another's *entry* into capitalist exchange relationships or to prevent another's *exit* into an altogether different economic system' and 'the latter appears to have driven a good deal of US imperialism after World War II'; furthermore, 'the onset of capitalist relations in the third world was also replete with the use of force'. But Marxist theories of neo-imperialism, neo-colonialism and 'underdevelopment' in the Third World also confront many difficulties, and the issues they raise will need to be considered later in the broader framework of an examination of Schumpeterian and other conceptions of the central themes and problems of economic sociology (in Chapter 8 below). For the moment we can say that Schumpeter's general theory of economic development was incomplete insofar as it did not provide anything like an adequate analysis of the causes, modes and consequences of the expansion of capitalism on a world scale.

The second major, explicitly sociological work that Schumpeter published in this period is his monograph on social classes (1927b). The basic idea, as he noted in the preface, was first presented in a lecture course at the University of Czernowitz in 1910/11, and subsequently developed in lectures at Columbia University in 1913/14. As published, the study formulated 'a line of reasoning' which, he said, 'I shall be able to work out fully only years from now, if at all' (p. 133). In fact he never did return to the subject, in spite of his insistence on its importance (p. 136), although according to Sweezy (1951, p. xi) it 'retained a place in his plan of work throughout the rest of his life – I have on several occasions heard him voice the intention to return to it some day'. Schumpeter (p. 134) also explicated the title of his monograph, 'Social classes in an ethnically homogeneous environment', by saying that this 'is not meant to deny the significance of racial differences in explaining concrete class formations'; on the contrary his 'early thinking on the subject followed the paths of the racial theory of classes' as expounded by Gumplowicz,[8] and was also influenced by the lectures of Haddon on racial types at the London School of Economics in 1906. Nevertheless, Schumpeter argued, 'this is not the heart of the matter, not the reason why there are social classes', and although racial factors are sometimes important it is proper, in 'investigating the "essential nature" of a social phenomenon', to ignore various external factors that may be quite common.

Schumpeter began his analysis by distinguishing four separate problems in class theory: (i) the *nature* of classes, and the function of class 'in the social whole'; (ii) class *cohesion*; (iii) class *formation*; and (iv) the *concrete causes and conditions* of an individually determined, historically given class structure (p. 139). One striking feature of his preliminary discussion of the characteristics by which a social class can be recognized is his abandonment of the 'methodological individualism' that he had lauded in his first book (1908; see above, page 19). Class, he argued, 'is something more than an aggregation of class members . . . a class is aware of its identity as a whole, sublimates itself as such, has its own peculiar life and characteristic "spirit" ' (p. 140). One symptom of class cohesion is 'the specific way in which people engage in social intercourse', and this is 'decisively influenced by the degree of "shared social *a priori*", as we might say with Simmel' (p. 141). Intercourse across class boundaries is difficult, and a criterion of class can be found 'in the fact that intermarriage prevails among its members, socially rather than legally' (p. 141).[9]

Thus Schumpeter, just like the Marxist thinkers, conceived

classes as 'collective subjects', but he diverged from Marxism (much more radically than did Max Weber, for example) in excluding from his analysis the social functions of classes (except in a very restricted sense), the relations between classes, and above all class conflict, which is only briefly mentioned on one or two occasions and then only to be dismissed (most inaccurately) as an idea which 'has fallen into discredit among the best minds in science and politics alike' (p. 139), or excluded from discussion (p. 211, footnote). His study, as he said (p. 142), applied primarily to the third of the problems he had distinguished – the formation of classes – and it can be seen, from one aspect, as a major exercise in consigning the Marxist theory of class to oblivion, which it was doubtless intended to do. Even as an analysis of the formation of classes, however, it has definite limitations, since Schumpeter excluded discussion of any original emergence of classes,[10] and began by postulating 'given class situations'. His further analysis is then concerned in fact with changes in class structure and class situations resulting from the rise and fall of families within a class, movement across class lines, and the rise and fall of whole classes. The first two of these themes do not strictly speaking concern class formation, but rather the composition, or membership, of a particular class, and Schumpeter's discussion allowed him to introduce the idea of superior abilities (of a family or individual) as a determinant of class position. Thus, he criticized Marx's view of the 'automatism' of capitalist accumulation by observing that 'the captured surplus value *does not invest itself* but must *be invested*'; and so we are led away 'from the *social* "force" to the *individual –* physical or family', and in some degree from the 'inner necessities of any given situation' to the factor of *individual disposition* (p. 155). Finally, in summarizing the argument of his monograph he concluded that 'the ultimate foundation on which the class phenomenon rests consists of differences in aptitude', but these differences are to be understood 'with respect to those functions which the environment makes "socially necessary" ', and furthermore they 'do not relate to the physical individual, but to the clan or family' (p. 210). It was also a necessary part of this argument that class barriers are not insurmountable, and that there is a continuous circulation of families between classes, and Schumpeter assembled some historical data to support this view, giving particular attention to a study of the origins of entrepreneurs in the

English cotton industry. 'The persistence of class position', he concluded, 'is an illusion, created by the slowness of change and the great stability of class character as such' (p. 170).

The idea expressed here is very similar to Pareto's conception of the 'circulation of elites', and in a later article, Schumpeter (1949) gave prominence to this aspect of Pareto's thought, at the same time comparing it with Marxism, to the disadvantage of the latter. Thus he argued that Pareto introduced important new elements into political sociology: the significance for historical explanation of 'the greater or smaller degree of social flexibility [especially with regard to vertical mobility and resistance to it] that a given society displays'; and a conception of the historical process as being 'not so much the result of the conflict of comprehensive social classes as it is the result of the conflict of their ruling minorities'. He then added that 'property relations *per se* are much less in evidence with Pareto than they are with Marx, and . . . this also constitutes a claim to superiority of the Paretian analysis' (pp. 140–1).

The similarity with Pareto's élite theory, and in particular with his conception of history as a 'graveyard of aristocracies', is very clear in that section of Schumpeter's monograph which deals with the 'rise and fall of whole classes'. What is most strongly emphasized in his analysis, however, is 'the connection between the social rank of a class and its function. Each class is always linked to such a special function. That is the real core of all theories of the division of labour and occupation in the field of class phenomena' (p. 179);[11] and he went on to argue that 'changes in relative class position are always explained' by 'the significance attributed to the function' and 'the degree to which the class successfully performs the function' (p. 180). In a brief historical survey he noted the predominance of the military function in European feudal society, and the related organization of the economy in great manorial estates, forming a class system which endured until the eighteenth century, 'even then leaving a heritage of established position to later times' (p. 184), as he had attempted to show more fully in the monograph on imperialism.

Nevertheless, Schumpeter argued that this dominant class, a military, landowning aristocracy, had been 'almost without interruption on the downgrade' from the end of the fourteenth century, not through a decline in its legal status or social position but by its gradual subjection to a new social factor, the centralized nation state (p. 189), relying on an administrative machine which 'could be – and was in fact – wrested from the grasp of the nobility and even of the sovereign' (p. 190). This is one of the very few references, in this instance only allusive, that Schumpeter made to the rise of a new class – the bourgeoisie – and his discussion of the 'rise and fall of whole classes' has the surprising characteristic that it is concerned almost exclusively with the 'fall', as will be seen again when we consider his later work (Schumpeter 1942), where it will also be necessary to examine further his view of the role of individuals – not implying 'the errors of individualism' (p. 211) – and of the function of 'social leadership' (p. 214). It is greatly to be regretted that Schumpeter did not pursue this study of social classes, after having declared in his prefatory note (p. 136) that 'the subject . . . poses a wealth of new questions, offers outlooks on untilled fields, foreshadows sciences of the future . . . [and] one often has a strange feeling, as though the social sciences of today, almost on purpose, were dealing with relative side-issues'; but its importance seems gradually to have faded in his thought, although some of its themes re-emerged, in provocative ways, later on. Had he ever returned to a systematic study of the subject he might have been led to revise radically his basic conceptions, or perhaps would only have presented an array of conflicting ideas, as he did on some other questions.

Besides the monographs on imperialism and on social classes Schumpeter also published in this period two other studies which have a sociological character and were included later in a volume of his essays on sociology (Schumpeter 1953). In the first of them, on the crisis of the 'tax state' (1918), he outlined a 'sociology of public finance' (or 'fiscal sociology') taking as his starting-point partly the widespread public discussion of a crisis in the finances of the state, exacerbated by the growth of public debt during the war, and partly the pioneering work of Goldscheid (1917) which had posed many issues and presented much material about the historical development of public finance that had now, in Schumpeter's view, to be brought into the domain of sociological enquiry. Much of the essay is devoted to an analysis of the scope and limits of both direct and indirect taxation,[12] and of the specific problems of post-war reconstruction in Austria, but Schumpeter also raised wider issues concerning the meaning and implications of a fiscal crisis, the close relation between the tax-state and the private enterprise economy (the former being the fiscal expression of a distinct type of society), which nevertheless included elements of incompatibility. And in the concluding pages he considered the possibility that in some future stage the private enterprise economy might be superseded, arguing first that this could not happen in a society which the war had impoverished and set back in its development (and Marx, he claimed, would have laughed uproariously at the idea), but that the time for it would come when, as a result of economic development and the extension of the range of social sympathy, private enterprise would lose its social meaning (Schumpeter, 1953, pp. 56–8). These general themes foreshadow Schumpeter's later studies of economic crises, and especially of capitalism and socialism, and I shall examine them further in that context.

In his other essay (1929), on the 'social physiognomy of Germany', Schumpeter was mainly concerned with analysing the changing class structure and its political implications, in a way that had some affinities with the ideas expounded earlier by Bernstein (1899), and by Karl Renner in various wartime and post-war writings, but already differed considerably from the analysis in his general study of classes published two years earlier. Any study of the 'spirit of a people', Schumpeter argued, must begin by recognizing the distinct viewpoints of different social strata, and he then proceeded to examine the effects of changes in social structure on these diverse cultural/political conceptions (Schumpeter, 1953, p. 215). The 'social pyramid' can be divided roughly into two economic spheres: the agricultural and the industrial. Here the first phenomenon to note is the movement of population, since 1871, from the countryside to the towns (p. 217). On the land itself, Schumpeter argued, the conflict between the higher and lower aristocracy, and more importantly, that between the aristocracy as a whole and the peasantry, had virtually ended, with the victory of the peasantry; and he went on to show the extent of small and medium-size peasant landholding. The peasant economy is sound, he concluded, and the peasantry had become the most conservative element in society. In the case of the industrial pyramid Schumpeter first observed that the pace of development of large enterprises and corporations had been exaggerated by public opinion, and that small producers and tradesmen still had an important place, though the latter faced growing economic difficulties (p. 221). An economic depression, however, would endanger all these small businesses, and lead to a decline of that 'bourgeois spirit' (p. 222) which he later argued was so essential to the survival of capitalism.

The most important 'power factor', however, was the industrial workers, and here Schumpeter noted particularly that while their numbers had grown only slowly between 1907 and 1925 (from 8.5 million to 9.8 million), nevertheless the working class had become unmistakably a 'homogeneous mass' whose social weight and influence must necessarily increase, though more in the direction of striving for a petty bourgeois style of life, he considered, than in any movement towards a radical transformation of society (p. 223). But the most dramatic of all changes had been the tremendous growth of the 'intellectual stratum' from about 300,000 in 1882 to an estimated 3.5 million in 1925. A more appropriate term for this social group would in fact be the 'intelligentsia' (in the sense of those who had had a fairly prolonged period of formal education), or 'new middle class', since Schumpeter included in it, as indeed its largest element, office workers (i.e. the white-collar middle class) who are indispensable for the modern economy – 'machines must not only be operated but administered, Taylorism requires office workers, etc.' (p. 223). This large stratum might or might not ally itself with the working class, but its continued growth would at all events ensure that 'the world of the future will, without doubt, be a world of bureaucracy' (p. 224).

It was certainly unfortunate that Schumpeter should have ended his essay by asserting the great, and possibly still increasing, stability of the social situation in Germany, and the opposition of an overwhelming majority of the population to any kind of extremist policy: 'In no sense, in no sphere, and in no direction are eruptions, sensational events, or catastrophes at all probable' (p. 225). For only two years later a profound economic crisis was devastating Germany, and the Social Democratic Party, which had been a major factor in the preceding stability, 'was locked in a life-and-death struggle with the National Socialists' (Braunthal 1967, vol. 2, p. 354). In mitigation, however, it should be said that Schumpeter did no worse than other economists and sociologists, none of whom foresaw, or perhaps *could* foresee, the world economic crisis or its particular character and outcome in Germany; so that a Marxist like Hilferding, who had become finance minister in the coalition government of 1928, also continued for a time to think in terms of a post-war stabilization of capitalism, although he resigned from the government at the end of 1929 after his fiscal proposals (which in retrospect appear eminently sensible and necessary) were rejected and there was external interference with his policies by the president of the Reichsbank (see Bottomore 1981, pp. 11–12). At all events, from 1930 onwards Schumpeter, who had already (1928b) written briefly on the longer-term 'instability of capitalism' (see above, page 39), devoted increasing attention to the subject of economic crises and cycles, and this work culminated in the publication of his next major study in 1939.

Finally we should consider the contribution to sociology made by the book on 'the phenomenon of money' (Schumpeter 1970), a first draft of which had been written by 1929, though not quite completed, or revised.[13] In Chapter 2 particularly, on the 'sociology of money', Schumpeter seemed to be proposing an analysis of money as a *social* phenomenon, since he began by observing that 'money, just like every other economic institution, is an element in the social process as a whole, and as such it is a concern of sociology, and indeed of historical, anthropological and statistical empirical research, as well as of economic theory' (p. 12). But his actual discussion is very disappointing, consisting largely of a review of historical writings on the early forms of money and speculations about its origins, without making any positive contribution of its own. What is most surprising is that there is no reference at all to Simmel's *Philosophy of Money* (1907), which is unquestionably one of the major contributions to the subject,[14] or to Hilferding's *Finance Capital* (1910), which was certainly an important influence on Schumpeter's own analysis of the role of the banks in 'money creation' (in Chapter 8, and previously in *The Theory of Economic Development*); and there are only a few minor and unimportant references to Weber (mainly to his *General Economic History* 1923). Even in the discussion of 'economic calculation in a socialist community' (Chapter 4), where Schumpeter takes a critical stance *vis-à-vis* Mises's (1920, 1922) arguments against socialism, there is little that is specifically sociological, and his analysis, concerned primarily with the economic problem of a rational combination of means of production, and of rational calculation more generally, in a centrally planned economy (pp. 98–102), is very similar to that which was later elaborated by Oskar Lange (1938). The sociological element in Schumpeter's book is, therefore, quite limited, being largely confined to the distinctions he made occasionally between different types of economy, to comments on historical studies of money, and to some rather vague general references to a broader 'social context'. It is understandable, I think, that he was dissatisfied with the book in its extant form, and reluctant to publish it, both in 1929 and in 1939; and its only value now is as a source of infrequent comments on money as a 'social phenomenon' which reappeared in some later writings, but were never developed more extensively.

In the title of this chapter I referred to Schumpeter's sociological 'excursions', but we can now see that in some of his works of the period from the end of the First World War to the late 1920s he was really aiming to achieve more than that, by developing a sociological approach which would give a particular character to his later studies. First, unlike most economists of his own time, or later, Schumpeter made a clear distinction between different kinds of economy, which are embedded in different types of society – feudal, capitalist, and in the future perhaps socialist. Secondly, he regarded these societies as having distinct class structures, in which particular social groups have a leading role and function – in feudal society a landowning armed aristocracy, in capitalist society the bourgeoisie and more specifically the entrepreneurs. Thirdly, he conceived each type of society and economy, but particularly capitalism, as undergoing change in the course of time (with some variations between individual countries) as a result of the impact of internal and external forces; and these cumulative changes over a long period may give birth to a new kind of society.

This sociology, it will readily be seen, was not only economic but also historical, concentrating upon endogenous sources of change, above all in the economy. In these respects it was very close to Marxist theory, as Schumpeter frequently recognized, and it also had important affinities with Max Weber's studies, though the latter were more profoundly sociological in their analysis of different social structures. But Schumpeter's own studies of the nature and development of capitalism diverged in major respects both from Marxist conceptions (incorporating indeed a well-informed critique of Marxism) and also from Weber's alternative interpretations. The substance of this attempt at a historical sociology of modern capitalism, its limitations, subsequent criticisms of it, and its relation to the theories of Marx and Weber in particular, form the main subject matter of the following chapters.[15]

Notes

1. First in the *Archiv für Sozialwissenschaft und Sozialpolitik* (vol. 46, pp. 1–39, 275–310) and then as a book in the same year.
2. Bukharin's book, *Imperialism and World Economy*, inspired by Hilferding's study and influencing Lenin (who read it in manuscript), though written in 1915 was not published in full until 1918.
3. This is very similar to Veblen's argument in *Imperial Germany and the Industrial Revolution* (1915) where the imperialism of Germany and Japan was explained by the fact that these empires, though technologically advanced, were still socially and ideologically 'feudal'. It seems unlikely, however, that Schumpeter had read Veblen's book at this time.
4. This idea of the inherently pacific nature of modern capitalism, or industrial society, goes back to Saint-Simon, Comte and Spencer, and their conception of history as a movement from 'military society' to 'industrial society'. See the illuminating discussion by Raymond Aron (1958), who noted the contrary prediction of Nietzsche that the twentieth century would be one of great wars, because 'urban mass civilizations are bellicose, not pacific, and the spread of Western civilization would offer the contending great powers an immense prize – world domination' (p. 6). Whether Schumpeter had read Saint-Simon, Comte or Spencer at the time of writing his monograph, or whether he was familiar with their ideas from some other source, such as Gumplowicz, whose works he knew while he was 'still at school' (Schumpeter 1927b, Prefatory note), is not clear, but at all events his own view is a curious 'survival' or revival of theirs. Much later, in his *History* (1954), Schumpeter did discuss Comte's work in some detail, as part of the 'intellectual scenery' of the period 1790–1870 (and also mentioned Spencer), but he concentrated on Comte's 'positivism', his distinction between static and dynamic analysis, and his general evolutionary scheme, without referring at all to the two types of 'military' and 'industrial' society.
5. Or even afterwards, so far as the character of 'popular beliefs' can be determined at all in a totalitarian system maintained by indoctrination

and repression. It was the large capitalists and landowners, a substantial part of the middle class and peasantry, and some of the unemployed workers, who mainly supported the fascist movement, while the oppositional working-class organizations were attacked and eventually destroyed.

6. The principal weakness of the German working class was not that it was seduced by imperialist ideas, but that its allegiance was divided between the SPD and the KPD; and that the policy of the latter, totally subservient to the Comintern in Moscow, involved concentrating its attacks on the SPD (defined as 'social–fascist') as the principal enemy (see Braunthal 1967, ch. 16; Beetham 1983, Introduction).

7. This distinction between rational and non-rational (or irrational) action had a prominent place in Schumpeter's discussion not only of the relation between imperialism and modern capitalism, but also of earlier forms of imperialism, and it may be that underlying his concept of 'social imperialism' there was a conviction that human behaviour is motivated less by rational aims than by non-rational impulses, as Winslow (1948, pp. 235–6) suggested. To the extent that Schumpeter did hold such a view, it is very probable that one major source was Pareto, whose work as an economist and sociologist he greatly admired (Schumpeter 1949). These more general questions will be discussed in Chapter 8 below.

8 Ludwik Gumplowicz (1838–1909) was the leading Austrian sociologist of the nineteenth century, and although his theory of social conflict in terms of races, nations and classes (against the background of nationalist struggles in the Habsburg Empire) was largely ignored or rejected in Austria, it had a considerable influence abroad, and he was sometimes regarded later on as one of the major 'founders' of sociology (see Mozetič 1985). Schumpeter's initial interest in his writings at the turn of the century might be considered somewhat eccentric, or even provocative, especially within the economics profession.

9. Schumpeter added that 'this criterion is especially useful for our purposes, because we limit our study to the class phenomenon in a racially homogeneous environment, thus eliminating the most important additional impediment to intermarriage'.

10. See his comments (p. 146, footnote) on the idea of an original 'classless society'.

11. Schumpeter noted earlier (p. 178) that war and conquest also bring about changes in the relative position of classes, but this is an external, 'accidental' influence on the existing class system.

12. Here and in later writings Schumpeter posed questions, and proposed courses of action, which are still relevant to modern discussions (Musgrave 1988, p. 275); and for example, a recent article (Prychitko

1990, pp. 623–5) has suggested a parallel to Schumpeter's study in the analysis by Offe (1984) of the problems of the present-day welfare state.
13. Its imminent publication was announced in 1929, and again, in an English version, in 1939, but it never appeared in Schumpeter's lifetime and was finally published in 1970, in an edition by Fritz Karl Mann, who also provided in his preface (pp. xxv-xxvii) a brief account of its publishing history.
14. Although it seems to me that there are in fact some faint echoes in Schumpeter's book of the general ideas which Simmel expounded in his preface (1907, pp. 53–6). On the other side, it is evident that in his discussion of value and money (1907, ch. 1) Simmel himself was much influenced by Austrian economic theory.
15. In this discussion I shall draw to some extent on a previous study (Bottomore 1985) in which I briefly compared the theories of capitalism expounded by Marx, Weber and Schumpeter, and considered some later phases of capitalist development.

CHAPTER 5

ECONOMIC CYCLES

The idea of economic cycles in a capitalist economy played an important part in Schumpeter's work from an early stage; as soon, in fact, as he had virtually abandoned 'static' or 'equilibrium' analysis. The final chapter of *The Theory of Economic Development* (1911, Chapter 6) was presented as a 'theory of crises, more correctly of recurrent business fluctuations', but it was still only a 'torso' and the subject required more exhaustive treatment (p. 212). In his preface to the English version of the book (1934) Schumpeter noted as one of its principal defects that he had taken for granted the existence of a single wave-like motion, whereas he now thought that there were at least three such movements, or 'probably more'; but he still considered that the outlines of his theory, and its results, were broadly correct (p. ix). The main theme of his analysis was the impact on the economic process of 'innovations' carried out by those he called 'entrepreneurs' (see above, page 32), and this theme was elaborated, explored historically, and set in a wider context, in a series of articles published from the later 1920s onwards, which led up to the comprehensive study of business cycles published in 1939.

This work, subtitled 'a theoretical, historical and statistical analysis of the capitalist process', can reasonably be regarded as a 'sociology of capitalism', in which the emphasis on the economy does not come so much from the natural preoccupations of one whose professional training had been primarily as an economist, as from the conviction that – as is asserted by the 'economic interpretation of history' – 'the economic world is relatively autonomous because it takes up such a great part of a nation's life, and forms or conditions a great part of the remainder' (1911, p. 58). This is stated more strongly, and in a specific form, in the first chapter of *Business Cycles* (1939, pp. 9–10) where Schumpeter, in considering how we should distinguish between external and internal causes of economic change, argued that the 'mechanization of industry' is *not* an external factor: 'we hold . . . (in this respect entirely agreeing with Marx) that technological progress was of the very essence of capitalist enterprise and hence cannot be divorced from it'.

In the following chapter Schumpeter proceeded to construct a model for analysing 'autonomous change in a closed domain', and in fact embodied in it hypotheses and assumptions which he claimed to exclude, one of them being that the analysis could most conveniently begin with 'the construction of the model of an unchanging economic process' as 'definitively achieved' by Walras (pp. 30–6). But this seems to have been more an act of piety than anything else, for in the following passage Schumpeter went on to say that 'the Walrasian or for that matter, Paretian or Marshallian description constitutes but a first approximation which stops far short of what we need for an analysis of processes in an incessantly disturbed economic world', and further, that 'later on we shall, of course, often meet with patterns of reality which require qualification, improvement, or even abandonment of that Walrasian model' (p. 47). In short, equilibrium analysis is neither necessary nor particularly useful for studying the real process of capitalist development, and Schumpeter's reference to it is an irrelevance.[1]

The main substance of the book is to be found in Schumpeter's analysis of the major internal factors of change in a capitalist economy – innovation and invention, the role of the entrepreneur, and credit creation by the banking system. Innovation was first defined very broadly to cover 'the introduction of new commodities . . . technological change . . . Taylorization of work, improved handling of material, the setting up of new business organizations . . . in short, any "doing things differently" in the realm of economic life' (p. 84). Schumpeter went on to point out that innovation is not synonymous with invention, and 'it is entirely immaterial whether an innovation implies scientific novelty or not' although in fact 'most innovations can be traced to some conquest in the realm of either theoretical or practical knowledge' (p. 85).

In sum, 'the making of the invention and the carrying out of the corresponding innovations are, economically and sociologically, two entirely different things' (p. 85). The broad range of phenomena denoted by the term 'innovation' can, however, be encompassed in a more concise formulation, and Schumpeter concluded by saying that 'we will simply define innovation as the setting up of a new production function' (p. 87). The next stage in his argument was to associate innovation with the function of the entrepreneur, as distinct from that of the head or manager of a firm run on established lines, and here he briefly noted (pp. 102–9) the main points of his earlier 'economic and sociological analysis of both types and both functions' (in *The Theory of Economic Development*, 1911, Chapters 2 and 4; see above, pages 31–2).

Schumpeter's theory of innovation and entrepreneurship has been very widely discussed, and quite frequently criticized, in recent years, especially in connection with his analysis of economic cycles, though also with reference to his view of the decline of capitalism which will be examined in the following chapter; and our consideration of it will be helped by looking first at the cyclical schema which he presented. In his earlier book (1911) he had discussed only one type of cycle, the so-called 'Juglar cycle' of 8 to 9 years' duration, but he now introduced two others, the 40-month 'Kitchin cycle' and the Kondratiev 'long wave'[2] of approximately 50 years (pp. 164–5), and then went on to consider various problems arising from the 'assertion or denial of the coexistence of several cyclical movements' (p. 166). His own view was formulated in three propositions:

> First, if innovations are at the root of cyclical fluctuations, these cannot be expected to form a single wavelike movement, because the periods of gestation and of absorption of the effects by the economic system will not, in general, be equal for all the innovations that are undertaken at any time. . . . Second, a statistical and historical picture of a movement displaying more than one cycle may result from the fact that successive cyclical units are not so independent of each other as we assumed . . . in constructing our model. . . . Major innovations hardly ever emerge in their final form or cover in one throw the whole field that will ultimately be their own. The railroadization, the electrification, the motorization of the world are instances. . . .Third, a sequence of cycles, whether independent of one another or not, may be the result of processes

which have also effects other than those which show in the cycles themselves. (pp. 166–8)

Railroadization offers an example: it requires time for the new opportunities of production to be developed, and still longer for populations to move, new cities to grow, and so on. The Industrial Revolution provides another example: 'it consisted of a cluster of cycles of various span that were superimposed on each other. But these together wrought a fundamental change in the economic and social structure of society' (p. 168).

Schumpeter concluded this outline of his model by saying that in adopting a three-cycle schema he was not formulating a new hypothesis to replace the single-cycle hypothesis, but simply making a decision, choosing a schema which he found 'useful in his own work and in marshaling his facts' (p. 170). That is to say, he was constructing a model in a neo-Kantian sense, in a manner which has some resemblance to Weber's use of 'ideal-types', also neo-Kantian in inspiration. Equipped with this model, which he made clear did not cover every kind of economic fluctuation (pp. 174–5), such as those produced by various 'external' factors, and after further discussion of 'time series', 'trends' and 'cycles', Schumpeter continued with a detailed historical–statistical study of cycles (mainly the 'long waves'), primarily in Britain, the USA and Germany, from 1787 to 1913 (Chapters 6 and 7), and again in the post-war period from 1919 to 1929 (Chapter 14) and through the world economic crisis from 1930 to 1938 (Chapter 15).

Schumpeter's book appeared at an unpropitious time for attracting the amount of attention and discussion which he had doubtless hoped for and expected. Economic recovery was well under way in the major capitalist countries, stimulated particularly by their rearmament programmes; the Second World War was just beginning; and it was followed by a period of sustained economic growth at exceptionally high rates, which was also characterized by such new phenomena as greatly increased state intervention in the economy, conceived in either Keynesian or socialist terms, and an extension of public ownership in some countries.[3] Only with the onset of a new recession in the 1970s, and the breakdown, in many capitalist countries, of what might be called a 'Keynesian consensus' or, alternatively, 'Fordism' or 'corporatism' (which I shall examine more fully in the next chapter), did Schumpeter's theory of cycles, and especially of long waves, evoke renewed interest and begin to be widely discussed;[4] and in the past decade or so a large literature on the subject has appeared.

An assessment of Schumpeter's theory, including the initial model, has to deal with two main questions: first, does it establish, with reasonable plausibility, the existence of regular wave-like fluctuations in a capitalist economy, and in particular of long waves; secondly, does it provide an *explanation* of these fluctuations? Many economists, of different persuasions, seem to have accepted the model in broad outline, though concentrating especially on the idea of long waves, but there has also been some more destructive criticism of it. One such critical study is that by Maddison (1982) who dismissed forthrightly the Kitchin and Juglar cycles, referring to 'Kitchin's paltry contribution to the literature' and declaring that 'Juglar never claimed to have demonstrated the existence of an eight- to nine-year rhythm' (p. 77). More generally he suggested that Schumpeter 'insisted on the empirical regularity of his schema as if the basic facts about these three cycles had been well established, whereas there are great doubts about all three', and furthermore, that he distinguished 'only the length of his three types of cycle', saying 'nothing about their amplitude', while his 'treatment of statistical material is illustrative rather than analytic and . . . at times rather cavalier' (*ibid.*). Another recent study (Reijnders 1990) also takes a somewhat sceptical view, observing that

> the question whether these [Kondratiev] waves are fact or phantasy, has still not yet been settled . . . [and] the fact that after such a long period this principal question has not been resolved, seems to indicate that the long wave is only an illusion. However, there remains the possibility that it is a reality after all. (p. xiii)

The focal point of Reijnders' study is a comparison of the methodological constructs, and the ensuing analysis, in the work of Kondratiev and Schumpeter, and I shall return to this subject later.

One feature of recent discussions is that the so-called 'Kitchin' and 'Juglar' cycles have been largely ignored, or at any rate accorded minor importance, while the long waves occupy the centre of the stage; and notwithstanding the scepticism I have noted, there are many writers who accept in principle the reality of such long-term cycles, though they may be more or less critical of various aspects of Schumpeter's analysis. The views of those who belong to what can be loosely described as 'mainstream economics' (though they form a deviant, neo-Schumpeterian stream within it, critical in many respects of neo-classical economics) have been expounded in a substantial literature emphasizing innovation and development, and I shall discuss some particular contributions later in considering the problems of explanation in long-wave theory. Not surprisingly, however, in the light of Marx's preoccupation with the economic crises of capitalism, long waves have also attracted the attention of some Marxist economists, and indeed Mandel has claimed that they were the first to develop the concept (see note 2 on page 83 below). Mandel's own study (1980) is a major contribution to a Marxist theory of long waves, which begins by asserting that 'the existence of these long waves in capitalist development can hardly be denied in the light of overwhelming evidence' (pp. 1–2). Similarly, another Marxist economist, Gordon (1980), though acknowledging the doubts about whether 'long cycles even exist', has nevertheless argued that 'sufficient regularity in the empirical pattern of capitalist growth and stagnation has been demonstrated' to justify a 'Kondratiev's wager' about their existence, and hence a conceptual reformulation of the Marxist notion of 'stages of capitalist accumulation' in order to clarify our understanding of them (pp. 10–11).

In what follows I shall make a similar 'Kondratiev's wager' as a basis for examining the problems that arise in attempting to provide a theoretical explanation, rather than an empirical description, or ideal-type conceptual model, of long waves. Maddison (1982, p. 79) posed several important issues, arguing that

> the main weaknesses of Schumpeter's long-wave theory (ignoring his failure to demonstrate their existence in the real world) are three-fold: (1) he does not explain why innovation (and entrepreneurial drive) should come in regular waves rather than in a continuous but irregular stream . . . (2) he makes no distinction between the lead country and the others, but argues as if they were all operating on a par as far as productivity level and technological opportunity is concerned . . . (3) he greatly exaggerates the scarcity of entrepreneurial ability and its importance as a factor of production.

Other critics have taken up these and additional 'vexed questions', as Gordon (1980, p. 10) noted:

> Why should long cycles recur? Why should they last roughly fifty years? What determines their amplitude? What is the connection between the sources of stagnation in one cycle and the innovations or events which stimulate recovery and a new burst of accumulation in the next?

The principal Marxist study of these issues is that by Mandel (1980), who observed in the first place that 'Marxists would refuse to follow those economic historians who centre their analysis of the long waves on price and money movements' (as Schumpeter largely did), but would start from the assumption that the basic laws of the capitalist system are those of capital accumulation; hence

> the key indicators of long waves are movements involving output of commodities and sales of commodities. And since Marx considered the world market to be the real framework of economic fluctuations, industrial output and statistics of world exports seem clearly to be the two key indicators. (p. 8)

Thus a long-term upsurge in industrial output expresses an increase in the rate of capital accumulation and the rate of profit, which make possible an upsurge of technological innovation, using newly available funds for investment and reserves of unapplied inventions. Mandel did not maintain, however, that an inner logic of the capitalist economy governed the whole long-wave movement (disagreeing in that respect with Kondratiev's conception of 'long cycles'), but argued that many non-economic factors, such as wars of conquest, class conflict, revolutions and counter-revolutions – in short, 'changes in the social environment in which capitalism operates' – play a major part in initiating an expansionist phase. Once this has occurred, however, 'the inner contradictions of the capitalist mode of production come into their own [and] it is inevitable that a new long wave of stagnating trend must succeed a long wave of expansionist trend' (p. 30). This introduction of external, 'accidental' (at least from the point of view of their timing) factors does undeniably bring an element of indeterminacy into the whole movement, not very different, it may be thought, from the indeterminacy of Schumpeter's sudden 'bunching' of technological inventions and innovations; and Mandel, in summarizing his view of long waves as representing distinct 'historical realities, segments of the overall history of the capitalist mode of production', argued that 'for that very same reason, they [i.e long waves] are of irregular duration' (p. 97). The answer to the question, why long waves should last approximately fifty years, is therefore that they do not. Hence their course cannot be exactly predicted, but only historically described, and in Mandel's view explained retrospectively by an analysis of the interplay between 'internal economic factors, "environmental" changes, and their mediation through socio-political developments' (p. 97).

A recent work by Reijnders (1990), after a useful introductory account of the development of long-wave research, is primarily concerned with methodological difficulties in the work of Kondratiev and Schumpeter, whose studies, in his view, failed to resolve the basic problem of separating 'cycles' from long-term 'trends' (characterized mainly by economic growth). In his final chapter, therefore, Reijnders makes use of a statistical model (outlined in the preceding chapter) that is capable of isolating the movements of the trend, and a spectral analysis, to study one national economy (Britain) over a long historical period. This analysis, he concludes, 'indicates that the explanatory power of the Kondratiev domain is relatively high especially with respect to indicators of aggregate activity such as gross national product and employment. Therefore the Kondratiev wave cannot be regarded as an illusion' (p. 241). But this conclusion has to be qualified in three ways: (i) 'the present results apply only to one single national entity [Britain] and this context is too limited for drawing far-reaching conclusions'; (ii) 'the present results have only an empirical status', but they may 'indirectly contribute to what will ultimately be the principal part of the validation of Kondratiev's findings: its explanation on a theoretical level'; (iii) 'the scope of the present results is not limited to Kondratiev waves alone. . . . If one decides to accept the Kondratiev wave . . . one will also have to accept that this particular movement is embedded in a rather complicated structure which contains a multitude of wavelike movements not only of shorter but also of considerably longer duration than the Kondratiev wave itself' (p. 242).

Assuming the validity of the statistical procedures that Reijnders employs, his results give some support to the contention that the Kondratiev waves are an identifiable real phenomenon, though they have to be seen as one element in a complicated movement which includes many different waves (as Schumpeter also proposed; see above, page 64). The next, most important step is to provide an explanation of the occurrence of long waves, and their duration. As we have seen, Mandel gave a Marxist explanation in terms of changes in the rate of capital accumulation and of surplus value and profit, but also made a distinction between 'long cycles' and 'long waves', the latter, because they are affected by shocks from outside the system, having a variable duration (see above, page 64). Schumpeter's explanatory scheme, if it can properly be called that rather than a 'conceptually clarified history' (1939, p. 220), looks very different. First sketched in 1911, it was presented more fully, with extensive historical documentation, in 1939, and during the past two decades it has come to occupy an important place in research and debate, particularly among the numerous 'followers' of Schumpeter, whose main preoccupations have been with the development and diffusion of technology, and with the processes of innovation (Reijnders 1990, p. 46; Hanusch 1988; Heertje and Perlman 1990). The theory, or conceptual scheme, has three principal elements: first, the advance of science and technology; second, the innovations in production which are stimulated primarily by this advance; and third, the entrepreneur who initiates and carries through the innovations.

Let us consider these three elements in turn. Among Schumpeter's many borrowings from Marxism the most fundamental was undoubtedly his 'vision' of the development of capitalist production, in an intimate relationship with the growth of science and technology, as the central issue for economic theory. Marx was unique among the social scientists of his time in the emphasis which he placed upon the creation of 'more colossal productive forces' and 'the subjection of nature's forces to man' (*Communist Manifesto*), and in his anticipation of an increasingly rapid advance towards a state of affairs in which 'social knowledge' and its application would become the vital productive force, and at the same time the precondition for the construction of a new kind of society (*Grundrisse*, pp. 592–4). Schumpeter, to be sure, made a

distinction between 'invention' and 'innovation', but he always treated the former as a prime mover, and his descriptions of the various Kondratiev cycles are formulated in terms of specific periods of technological progress – the first industrial revolution, railways, electrification, motorization. Similarly, perhaps, we might describe the post-1945 cycle as that of nuclearization and computerization (or the massive surge of information technology which Marx, in very general terms, foresaw).

But the depiction of these long waves as a phenomenon arising from technological invention, its impact upon the organization of production, the subsequent 'routinization' of the innovations, and the onset of a period of stagnation and decline (though from a new level of economic productivity), still does not explain their periodicity, or establish causal links between the various phases. It poses a theoretical problem, not a solution. Both Marx and Schumpeter regarded the process of capitalist production as one which was turbulent and discontinuous. But Marx, to the extent that he formulated a systematic conception of economic cycles or crises at all, thought in terms of ten-year cycles (Bottomore 1985, pp. 11–12); and on the other hand he seems implicitly to have conceived the development of science and technology as a cumulative and continuous, though accelerating, process. Schumpeter, on the contrary, focused his attention on the long waves (into which the shorter cycles were to be fitted), and claimed to show that the expansionist phase of such waves was set off by a burst of major inventions and innovations which he later referred to as 'a gale of creative destruction' (1942, Chapter 7). Nowhere, however, did he explain why these 'gales' should occur at intervals of approximately fifty years, and his conception of the process of innovation, which remained an intuitive idea, never empirically tested, has been the object of much subsequent criticism.

Even those who are in general favourably disposed towards Schumpeter's cyclical scheme, as providing an illuminating model, have been highly critical of its theoretical significance. In the view of Tichy (1984, p. 83), 'one could say that Schumpeter neither had an explicit theory of invention, nor an explicit theory of innovation, nor an explicit theory of diffusion of technical progress and of innovation'. Similarly, Freeman (1990, p. 22) observed that Schumpeter 'scarcely discussed the origins of innovation, had virtually nothing to say about the interactions of science and technology, and largely neglected the cumulative nature of technology', and went on to cite the earlier pungent comment by Ruttan (1959):

Neither in *Business Cycles* nor in Schumpeter's other work is there anything that can be identified as a theory of innovation. The business cycle in Schumpeter's system is a direct consequence of the appearance of clusters of innovations. But no real explanation is provided as to why innovations appear in clusters or why the clusters possess the particular types of periodicity which Schumpeter indentified.

To some extent, it is clear, Schumpeter deliberately eschewed any attempt to provide a theoretical explanation. In a revealing footnote (1939, p. 405, n. 1), after referring to Hilferding's *Finance Capital* and presenting what he called 'a rough statement of the Neo-Marxist [i.e. Austro-Marxist] theory of the imperialist stage of capitalist evolution', he continued thus:

> since the cyclical process is not an incident but the whole of what is specifically capitalistic in economic life, it would really be our duty to enter upon a discussion of that theory, and either to accept it or to develop a theory of our own, elements of which are, in fact, implied in the construction of our model. But this cannot be done within the frame of the present work, into which the device of operating by 'external factors' has been introduced precisely in order to exclude those deeper problems and to concentrate attention on a more restricted task.

There were also particular features of Schumpeter's general approach which distracted his attention from the central theoretical problems. One was his obstinate attempt to reconcile or amalgamate business-cycle analysis with equilibrium analysis, which many later commentators have regarded as a more or less fruitless diversion (Tichy 1984, p. 82; Goodwin 1990, pp. 39–40). More important, however, was his concentration on the entrepreneur as the essential agent of innovation. In his first exposition of the theory of economic development Schumpeter conceived the entrepreneur as an individual person, saying that 'the carrying out of new combinations we call "enterprise"; the individuals whose function it is to carry them out we call "entrepreneurs" ' (1911, p. 74). This conception is largely assumed throughout his discussion of business cycles, but at the same time there are suggestions of an entirely different view in which, so to speak, a 'collective entrepreneur' emerges onto the stage. This alternative view is apparent not only in his comments on monopoly and oligopoly – for example in his observation (1939, p. 91) that 'the firms which

... are upsetting existing industrial structure and, as it seems, heading towards monopoly, are in general precisely those which have set up new production functions', and his reference to 'giant concerns which often are but shells within which an ever-changing personnel may go from innovation to innovation' (p. 96) – but also in his discussion of innovation in a socialist society, carried out by a central planning authority (pp. 111–12). However, it was only somewhat later, in *Capitalism, Socialism and Democracy*, that Schumpeter placed the 'collective entrepreneur' (a term which he never used, having no doubt an innate aversion to such an expression) firmly at the centre of the process of innovation, arguing that in our epoch large-scale enterprises or units of control have come to be the most powerful engine of economic progress, not only emerging and developing in the process of creative destruction but largely creating the conditions which they exploit (1942, Chapter 8; see also Hammond 1984).

We have to deal, therefore, with two kinds of problem in seeking an explanation of the cyclical nature of economic development as Schumpeter analysed it. If the entrepreneur is conceived as an individual person we must ask why there should be a 'swarming' of such individuals in particular periods, and furthermore, why their activities should subsequently diminish again in the depressive phase of the cycle. If, however, we think in terms of a collective entrepreneur – a giant corporation or a central planning authority – we need to ask why *their* innovatory activity should be supposed to occur in periodic spasms rather than as a continuous process, which seems a more plausible hypothesis in an age which has seen an increasingly close relationship between science and production and a massive growth of R&D departments in large corporations. Underlying both problems is a further question about the periodicity of scientific/technological inventions themselves, which are the main driving force in the process of innovation. It may well be argued that *major* scientific discoveries occur in 'leaps', and that a fairly long period of time is needed for their technological applications to work themselves out fully, but it is not at all clear why such advances should take place every fifty years or so; and in the present state of science one might indeed expect to see a more continuous and cumulative kind of development becoming established.

Schumpeter, as many later writers have observed, did not

attempt to resolve such questions. His study was devoted to demonstrating, by the compilation of statistical and historical data, the empirical reality of three significant cyclical movements, and especially the long waves, and to constructing a model, or 'conceptually clarified' historical scheme (in which the somewhat obscure figure of the entrepreneur had a central place) which would at least illuminate some aspects of these movements. There is no doubt that his model is illuminating, and certainly provocative, since it has inspired much of the recent revival of interest in the diffusion of technology, long waves and economic development, but it is only the first step towards an explanation of these phenomena.

One attempted explanation, mentioned earlier (page 68 above), is that propounded by Mandel (1980), whose theory of economic cycles, including the long waves, takes as its starting-point Marx's basic proposition concerning the tendency of the average rate of profit to fall. Marx, as I have indicated, was primarily interested in cycles of approximately ten years (a period he assumed to be necessary for the renewal of fixed capital), as well as in the ultimate fate of the capitalist mode of production (which gave rise to the later 'breakdown' controversies). Mandel took account of the ten-year cycles, but proposed also to introduce a further time-frame encompassing the long waves. The differences between these two cycles can be stated briefly by saying first, that whereas in the ten-year cycle the renewal of fixed capital (investment) takes place at the existing level of technology or at a level which has been gradually and cumulatively improved, in the long wave it involves a much more radical restructuring of production as a result of major technological advances; and secondly, that while the ten-year cycles can be explained largely by factors inherent in the economic system, an explanation of the expansive phase of the long waves, according to Mandel, must give great weight to the impact of exogenous, non-economic 'shocks' (for which reason the time-frame of the long waves is variable).

Schumpeter's model excludes such Marxist conceptions – which are both economic and sociological – of the process of capitalist production as a whole, and the kind of analysis based upon them. Nevertheless, there are some affinities, which are more evident in Schumpeter's earlier book (1911, in the revised Chapter 6 of the English edition 1934), where he claimed to explain business cycles 'solely by an objective chain of causation which runs its course automatically' (p. 213), and summarized his conclusion by saying that

> the boom (which is now explained) creates out of itself an *objective situation*, which, even neglecting all accessory and fortuitous elements, makes an end of the boom, leads *easily* to a crisis, *necessarily* to a depression, and hence to a temporary position of relative steadiness and absence of development. (p. 236)

He then explained the features of the depression, which 'now appear as parts of a single causal nexus', by the fact that

> the boom itself of necessity causes many businesses to run at a loss, causes a fall in prices apart from that due to deflation, and in addition causes deflation through credit contraction [and] further, the diminution of capital investment and entrepreneurial activity, and hence stagnation in the industries producing means of production . . . are all explained. (p. 237)

This explanation is not so very distant from a Marxist analysis in terms of the falling rate of profit, overproduction, and a disproportion between the two sectors of production, of producer goods and consumer goods, aspects of which were elaborated by Mandel (1980; see page 68 above); and Schumpeter's major divergence, aside from his heavily qualified references to possible states of equilibrium, lies in his elevation of the entrepreneurs, and their periodic emergence in 'swarms' (like bees), to the status of a major causal factor in the onset of the boom. *Business Cycles* adds very little to this theoretical explanation, but tends rather to obscure and weaken it. Its main contribution is to expound more fully a three-cycle model of economic development, and to provide a detailed historical description of cyclical phases; after which the book ends weakly and unsatisfactorily (as if the author had become weary of the subject) without any attempt to restate the theory or to assess the degree of confirmation provided by the preceding laborious compilation and analysis of his historical material. All this contrasts strongly with the incisively argued concluding chapter of *The Theory of Economic Development*.

The main question we have now to consider is whether Schumpeter's most original contribution to economic thought – namely, his conception of the historically decisive role of the entrepreneur in the development of capitalism – has the theoretical significance which he attributed to it. I shall argue here that it has not. In the first place, he never defined the entrepreneur in a precise or adequate way, but in effect simply posited the existence of such a person as the economic actor who carries out 'new combinations' or 'innovations'. Entrepreneurs, he claimed, are 'a special type' (1911, p. 81), engaging in conduct which 'is accessible in very unequal measure and to relatively few people, so that it constitutes their outstanding characteristic' (p. 81, n. 2), and in the continuation of this long footnote he elaborated his argument in terms which are unmistakably those of Pareto's theory of élites. But he did not attempt to specify the particular qualities of the entrepreneur, to provide evidence of their limited distribution, or to show how these qualities had attained their great economic and social importance, and he was indeed hostile to such kinds of analysis. Thus in discussing the historical problem of the 'rise of capitalism' (1939, p. 228), he insisted that

> there is no need to speak, as Sombart and others did, of a new 'spirit' (*Geist*) having come about somewhere in the stretch between 1400 and 1600 to make people think and behave differently, or of the rise of a new economic system fundamentally different from the preceding one. In particular there is no need to trace what that group of authors entirely unrealistically considers as a new rationalism on one hand and as a new attitude toward profits on the other hand, to religious changes (M. Weber) – which is a way of arguing hardly superior to the economic interpretation of history which it was intended to improve or to replace.

But Schumpeter's own brief sketch of the gradual emergence of capitalism as a historically continuous process, which ignores so many significant aspects of the phenomenon, falls far short of being the 'conceptually clarified history' at which he aimed, and is in every respect much inferior to Weber's *General Economic History*, as well as to the historical analyses of Marx and some later Marxists. Furthermore, it contradicts to some extent his own earlier account of the rationality of capitalism (see page 37 above and the discussion in Chapter 8 below, pp. 126–9).

The shadowy figure of the entrepreneur becomes still more obscure when we consider the views that Schumpeter expressed about the role of large corporations in the process of innovation. Already in 1928, in his article on 'the instability of capitalism', he had noted the change brought about by 'trustified' capitalism (which he also referred to elsewhere as 'organized capitalism', following Hilferding's usage). In this new historic type of capitalism

> innovation is . . . not any more embodied *typically* in new firms, but goes on, within the big units now existing, largely independently of individual persons . . . [it] tends to be carried out as a matter of course on the advice of specialists . . . [and] conscious policy towards demand and taking a long-time view towards investment becomes possible . . . credit creation still plays a role [but] the power to accumulate reserves and the direct access to the money market tend to reduce [its] importance. (1928b, p. 70)

An analysis of this kind of innovation, in particular, requires, as many later commentators have observed (e.g. Hammond 1984, pp. 41–2; Freeman 1990, p. 26), a theory of the firm rather than a theory of the entrepreneur (even a 'collective entrepreneur'), and I shall return to this subject later.

Meanwhile, however, we should note a further complexity in Schumpeter's conception which leads to an apparent contradiction. For on the one hand he emphasized the role of the large-scale enterprise as the most important innovator (i.e. entrepreneur) in trustified capitalism, while on the other hand he also interpreted the development and the economic dominance of large corporations as a process in which the entrepreneur would ultimately disappear, thus undermining the whole capitalist order. The latter argument was most fully expounded in his later book, *Capitalism, Socialism and Democracy* (1942), and I shall examine it in detail in the next chapter.

For the present we can say that Schumpeter's model of the capitalist economy incorporated the following five characterstics: (i) capitalism is a dynamic economic system which itself 'generates the force which incessantly transforms it' (1937 preface to Japanese edition of Schumpeter 1911, in English in Schumpeter 1951, p. 159); (ii) this development does not take place smoothly and continuously, but through a turbulent process of 'creative destruction'; (iii) the phases of rapid growth are those in which major innovations have a sudden and explosive impact on the production functions; (iv) the primary source of these innovations is the advance of science and technology; (v) the translation of science-based technological achievements into innovations is the function of an entity (individual, or possibly collective) called the entrepreneur. Clearly, this model diverged widely from the one employed in equilibrium analysis, and in this sense (as well as in respect of the greater importance that he attached to historical and sociological analysis) Schumpeter was a major critic of his immediate predecessors, the neo-classical economists, and the originator of a radically different theoretical scheme. But he was not, to the same extent, a critic of Marx or of the later Austro-Marxist school. On the contrary, the first four elements of his model, as I have set them out above, are very close to Marx's theory, except that Marx attached even greater importance to the progress of science and technology, and foresaw (as Schumpeter did not) the advent of a knowledge-based economy such as is rapidly becoming established in the advanced industrial countries in this last decade of the twentieth century, though he was less successful in predicting the social consequences of this process.

It should be added that Schumpeter's distinction between the two historic eras of 'competitive capitalism' and 'trustified capitalism', outlined in 1928 and restated in 1942 in the course of his reconsideration of the nature and significance of entrepreneurship, also owed a great deal to the work of the Austro-Marxists. At the same time, however, his preoccupation with the role of the entrepreneur as innovator was a feature which particularly distinguished his model of the capitalist economy from that of Marx, and was the basis for one of his major criticisms of Marx's theory. In *Business Cycles*, after stating his assumption that 'innovations are always associated with the rise to leadership of New Men' (p. 96), Schumpeter went on to argue that there exists 'in the institutional pattern of capitalism', and indeed as 'an essential characteristic of it', machinery (i.e. the provision of bank credit) which enables individuals

> to function as entrepreneurs without having previously acquired the necessary means. It is leadership rather than ownership that matters. The failure to see this and, as a consequence, to visualize clearly entrepreneurial activity as a distinct function *sui generis*, is the common fault of both the economic and the sociological analysis of the classics and of Karl Marx. (pp. 103–4)

But this is not a very cogent criticism of Marx, who, it can be argued, simply took for granted the existence of entrepreneurs in a capitalist economy, and explained their innovative activity in a distinctive way. For Marx, every owner of means of production employing wage-labour, regardless of how he had obtained the necessary funds (inherited wealth, especially land ownership, money acquired through trade, savings or bank credit), was necessarily an innovator, for two main reasons inherent in the logic of the capitalist economy. First, each individual owner of capital, as a representative of capital in general, was driven to reduce the cost of labour power by every possible innovatory means, in order to increase the rate of surplus value and the accumulation of capital. Secondly, competition among capitalists forced every producer to reduce costs of production, lower the price or improve the quality of products, introduce new products, in order to retain or enlarge his share of the market. And in the background, enabling capitalist production to develop in this fashion, was the cumulative, and periodically dramatic, growth of science and technology. Of course Marx recognized that some capitalists were more successful than others – which might be a consequence of greater competence and determination, larger initial resources, sheer luck or other factors – but he also drew the conclusion that beyond a certain stage of development the larger producers would inevitably drive out, absorb or subordinate many smaller ones, and he did not have to resort to a vague notion of 'new men', or of a small élite of individuals possessing 'super-normal intelligence and energy', in order to explain this phenomenon, as Schumpeter did (1942, p. 16). Thus Marx, and later Marxists, focused attention upon an essential feature in the later development of capitalism – the growth of giant corporations, or the centralization and concentration of capital – to which Schumpeter gave only belated and inadequate recognition, even then depending largely upon the analyses made by Hilferding in *Finance Capital* (1910) and in subsequent studies of 'organized capitalism' (Hilferding 1927).[5]

One conclusion which can be drawn from this critical assessment is that Schumpeter, at the time when he was writing *Business Cycles*, was still insufficiently sociological in his approach, notwithstanding the fact that he referred occasionally to the impact of external shocks such as war, and more frequently, in the historical chapters, to the broader social framework in which economic development occurred. Thus he noted that in the second long wave (1843–97) – the outstanding feature of which was the 'railroadization of the world' – the state, in some continental European countries, played an important role (p. 346), and in analysing the initial phase (1898–1913) of the third long wave he argued that the whole social atmosphere had begun to change with the revival of protectionism, increased expenditure on armaments, a new spirit in fiscal and social legislation, the rise of political radicalism and socialism, and the growth of trade unionism, concluding that 'the deepest problem of the economic sociology of our epoch is whether those tendencies . . . were not fundamentally one, and whether they grew out of the very logic of capitalist evolution, or were distortions of it traceable to extra-capitalist influences' (p. 399). But he did not pursue these larger issues, and later, in discussing the problems of the post-war period (1919–29), he declared that 'the formidable task of interpreting, economically and sociologically, our own time cannot be attacked in this book'; yet he was still tempted to

> glance at the social process as a whole and in so doing adopt the convenient, though possibly inadequate, hypothesis of Marxism, according to which social, cultural, political situations and the spirit in which and the measures by which they are met, derive from the working of the capitalist machine (pp. 695–6)

and in the following few pages sketched some of the themes, and notably that of the decline of the bourgeois class, which were to be elaborated in his next major work. This is yet another indication of how Schumpeter, in grappling with major problems in his analysis, was continually forced to invoke the aid of Marxist theory to sustain his argument.

At the stage he had reached in 1939, however, Schumpeter was still clinging mainly to his original entrepreneurial model of capitalist development, the deficiencies of which have become increasingly apparent. There is little reason to believe any longer that the individual entrepreneur is either such a rare phenomenon, or on the other hand such a potent factor in innovation, as this model presupposes. It is the firm, whether an established business or a new one, which innovates (more or less continuously in minor ways, and periodically, if the cyclical model is correct, in major ones); and to an increasing extent this process is carried on by large corporations. Thus, in the expansionist long wave that began after 1945, which I have suggested might be described as the era of nuclearization and computerization (though it also had other important features such as the massive growth of the car industry, of air travel and aircraft construction, and of mass consumption in many fields), it is evident that innovation has been undertaken primarily by corporations, aided very often by government planning and support, while in some major areas – military technology and space exploration – much of the effort is directly initiated and managed by government agencies.

In short, the past four decades have seen the maturation of fundamental structural changes in the capitalist economy, which Schumpeter only later began to analyse more profoundly, and then in the specific context of what he conceived as the 'decline of capitalism'. He was hindered particularly in this reorientation of his analysis by a lingering attachment (alongside his declared commitment to the idea of impersonal forces operating in the economy) to an economic version of the 'great man' conception of history, which expressed his partiality for individualism in something more than a purely methodological sense, and had affinities both with Pareto's élite theory and with Weber's idea of the 'charismatic leader'. But just as the interpretation of history in terms of outstanding individuals is quite inadequate to explain major historical transformations of human society, so too, in a narrower sphere and even more obviously, is it impossible to explain the development of the capitalist economy solely, or even to any significant degree, by the activities of a small number of individual entrepreneurs endowed with supernormal abilities.

In order to establish even the rudiments of an explanatory scheme, what is essential is a much broader kind of enquiry into the social context in which science, technology and innovation develop and have their effects upon the economy. That is to say, we need to study, first, how institutionalized science advances (the 'social relations of science'), then the ways in which scientific discoveries are turned into technological inventions, and finally the routes and mechanisms by which these inventions (or more generally the progress of science) become embodied in innovations that change both the methods and the content of production. From the standpoint of economic sociology it is this third process which has a salient importance, and several recent writers – reassessing Schumpeter's work in the light of subsequent economic development – have proposed replacing his conception of the individual entrepreneur by that of an *entrepreneurial function* which is performed by firms rather than individuals, and have gone on to argue that the outstanding requirement, if we are to attain a better understanding of the process of innovation, is a more adequate theory of the firm (Hammond 1984, pp. 41–2).

The construction of any such theory, however, is a complex undertaking, reaching far beyond an abstract model of some presumed 'typical' firm. It involves an analysis of different types of firm, in different branches of production and differing in size, both publicly and privately owned, and situated in countries which have very diverse socio-economic systems, or else operating on an international level. Beyond that, if we want to identify more clearly the driving force, and the cyclical character, of economic development, we must also examine the role of governments in managing – and sometimes partially planning – the economy; the diverse and changing forms of the capitalist economy; and the particular features of socialist, or partly socialist, economies. Furthermore, in constructing this theory – perhaps more accurately designated as a theoretical model from which explanations may eventually be derived – we should not ignore the fact that a considerable economic space still exists in advanced capitalist countries (and also existed to some extent in the former communist countries of Eastern Europe) for small firms in which an individual performs at least a major part of the entrepreneurial function, and that more generally individual achievements in science, technology and the process of innovation may still have significant economic and social effects, however much they depend upon an accumulation of previous work and on the existence of an extensive institutional framework which sustains scientific and technological research and ensures the wide diffusion of knowledge necessary for innovation. In some spheres, during the past few decades – in the provision of new leisure facilities or of new consumer goods, for example, but perhaps more conspicuously in the sphere of property speculation and financial dealings – individuals have been able to create new firms, some of which, in due course, may themselves become corporations or be absorbed by existing corporations. But the role of small firms and small-scale entrepreneurs should not be exaggerated. The main contours of post-war economic development have been determined, and are increasingly determined, by the manufacturing and marketing activities of large corporations, by large financial institutions, and by various forms of economic intervention by the state, and it is these modes of collective action which must be a central concern of any new theory of the firm, of innovation and of economic fluctuations.

Such issues, it is clear, were not at the heart of Schumpeter's study of business cycles, although he made some passing references to them. Only in his next book, to which I shall now turn, did he try to bring together, in a comprehensive study of modern capitalism and its socialist alternative, a broad range of issues either touched upon or more closely analysed in many earlier writings, with the intention of providing a new synthetic view of the latest phase of economic development.

Notes

1. Yet he was still at this time bewitched by it, remarking again later (p. 69) that 'the concept of a state of equilibrium, although no such state may ever be realized, is useful and indeed indispensable . . . as a point of reference . . . fluctuations must be fluctuations around something'. This is not the case, however. All we need in order to depict a cycle, or wave-like motion, is knowledge of its state at different points in a time sequence, and any concept of equilibrium is otiose. Eventually, a few years later (1942, pp. 79–80), Schumpeter made a single brief reference to the concept in terms which suggest that he may finally have liberated himself from it.
2. As Schumpeter noted (p. 164), it was Kondratiev who 'brought the phenomenon fully before the scientific community [and] systematically analyzed all the material available to him on the assumption of the presence of a Long Wave, characteristic of the capitalist process', although he had had some precursors, and according to Mandel (1991, p. 324) 'the theory of long waves of economic development . . . was initiated by Marxist economists like Parvus (Helphand) and van Gelderen at the beginning of the twentieth century'. But see also Reijnders (1990, ch. 1) who discusses the precursors more fully and notes especially the important influence of Tugan-Baranowsky.
3. These were phenomena that Schumpeter (1950; see Chapter 6, note 1) was only able to analyse briefly in his last essay, dealing with what he termed 'the march into socialism'; a text which I shall discuss in the next chapter in the context of his other writings on capitalism and socialism.

4. One indication of this interest being the first reprinting of his book in 1982.
5. In a comment on Marx's explanation of the concentration of capital Schumpeter (1942, p. 33) observed only that 'this is much like what the current textbook says on the matter, and not very deep or admirable in itself'. But how did it get into the textbook? At all events Schumpeter went on to concede (p. 34) that 'to predict the advent of big business was, considering the conditions of Marx's day, an achievement in itself', enhanced by a correct perception of some of the consequences of that change.

CHAPTER 6

CAPITALIST DEVELOPMENT AND DECLINE

Schumpeter's thought, like the capitalist economy upon which it was directed, manifested a trend of development, in which from time to time there appeared new intellectual 'combinations'. The particular course that it would follow was set initially by his innovative book of 1911 expounding a distinctive theory of capitalist economic development; and over the next thirty years this theory was elaborated, extended to cover new phenomena and new areas of social analysis (which also entailed some important revisions of it), and finally given quite a different orientation. In *Capitalism, Socialism and Democracy* (1942, 6th edition 1987)[1] Schumpeter's principal subject was no longer the cyclical evolution of capitalism, but its progressive decline and the advent of socialism; and his thesis, boldly stated in the preface, though subsequently heavily qualified,[2] was 'that a socialist form of society will inevitably emerge from an equally inevitable decomposition of capitalist society' (1942, p. 409). Schumpeter also said of this volume that it was 'the result of an effort to weld into readable form the bulk of almost forty years [of] thought, observation and research on the subject of socialism' (p. 409), and its origins can therefore be traced back to his encounter with Austro-Marxism in 1905–6, from which stemmed his lifelong preoccupation with a social theory that he considered to have a 'unique importance'.

Thus he began his book with a comprehensive critical examination of Marx's thought, and of some later Marxist conceptions, which he had previously discussed only in brief commentaries (e.g.

1914b, pp. 119–24, 138–9; and 1919, pp. 104–11), had merely mentioned, or on a few occasions had excluded from consideration as lying outside his immediate subject matter. The framework of Marx's theory, Schumpeter argued, is constituted by the 'economic interpretation of history', and the content of the theory may be put into two propositions: (i) 'the forms or conditions of production are the fundamental determinants of social structures which in turn breed attitudes, actions and civilizations'; and (ii) 'the forms of production themselves have a logic of their own; that is to say, they change according to necessities inherent in them so as to produce their successors merely by their own working'. But although 'both propositions undoubtedly contain a large amount of truth and are . . . invaluable working hypotheses' (p. 12), the question may be posed whether the theory is more than a 'convenient approximation', and Schumpeter noted two important qualifications of the main thesis. First, he maintained:

> Social structures, types and attitudes are coins that do not readily melt. Once they are formed they persist, possibly for centuries, and . . . we almost always find that actual group and national behaviour more or less departs from what we should expect it to be if we tried to infer it from the dominant forms of the productive process.

Secondly, in the case of the origins of feudalism, he noted:

> the emergence of the feudal type of landlordism in the kingdom of the Franks during the sixth and seventh centuries . . . was certainly a most important event that shaped the structure of society for many ages and *also influenced conditions of production.* . . . But its simplest explanation is to be found in the function of military leadership previously filled by the families and individuals who (retaining that function however) became feudal landlords. (pp. 12–13)[3]

I shall return in a later discussion to consider the significance of these qualifications, and more particularly the first of them, but for the present we may note that Schumpeter raised here a fundamental question about the scope and adequacy of Marx's theory of history which has also, in recent years, preoccupied many Marxist historians and social theorists (see, for example, Shaw 1978, Habermas 1979, Larrain 1986), and poses issues that are of central importance in defining the field of economic sociology (see Chapter 8 below).

In this theory of history, however, there is another major

element – the theory of classes and class conflict – which Schumpeter also considered an important contribution, observing that 'Economists have been strangely slow in recognizing the phenomenon of social classes . . . [whose] existence entails consequences that are entirely missed by a schema which looks upon society as if it were an amorphous assemblage of individuals or families' (pp. 13–14). But he went on to criticize Marx's theory, initially with respect to 'primitive accumulation' (i.e. the origins of capitalism), from the standpoint of his own conception of classes, as expounded in 1927, claiming that 'supernormal intelligence and energy account for industrial success and in particular for the *founding* of industrial positions in nine cases out of ten' (p. 16) and reaffirming his view of 'the salient point about classes – the incessant rise and fall of individual families into and out of the upper strata' (p. 18). He did not, however, undertake any serious historical study of the class structure in search of evidence for these contentions, and modern sociological research on social mobility (Heath 1981) and on the extent to which wealthy families maintain their position in the capitalist class over very long periods (Scott 1982, 1991; Bottomore and Brym 1989) simply contradicts his assertion of an 'incessant rise and fall'. In his concluding remarks on class theory Schumpeter then produced the amazing contention that socialism 'in reality has nothing to do with the presence or absence of classes' (p. 19), which ignores the whole history of the working-class movement and a major part of the political conflicts characterizing the second half of the nineteenth century and the first half of the twentieth century. It also appears to discard the idea of the importance of 'the rise and fall of whole classes' in the development of society, expounded in his monograph of 1927, and differs greatly from his more empirical account (1929) of class structure in Germany (see above, page 55). But there is something cryptic and obscure in Schumpeter's statement, and I shall try to elucidate it further in the next chapter, in discussing his conception of socialism.

From this critical examination of Marx's sociological theory of capitalist society and its class system, Schumpeter proceeded to an assessment of the economic theory which in his view provided the 'mechanics' of the capitalist process of development (p. 20), and while criticizing from one aspect its basis in the labour theory of value, and the derived theory of surplus value (or 'exploitation'), he also emphasized its great importance in another context. Thus he argued that while 'at the ordinary level of the theory of a stationary economic process it is easy to show that under Marx's own assumptions the doctrine of surplus value is untenable', and the labour theory of value could 'never be applied to the production of the commodity labour' itself (p. 27), but nevertheless went on to say, in discussing the problem of the relation between values and prices, that 'it is not absurd to look upon surplus value as a "mass" produced by the social process of production considered as a unit and to make the rest a matter of the distribution of that mass' (p. 29, n. 9). His principal argument in support of Marx's economic theory, however, was that Marx did not aim at analysing a state of equilibrium, 'but on the contrary a process of incessant change in the economic structure' (p. 28), and that he 'saw this process of industrial change more clearly and he realized its pivotal importance more fully than any other economist of his time' (p. 32). One major feature of this process of change which Marx also clearly recognized was the centralization and concentration of capital – the advent of big business – and this played an important part in Schumpeter's own theory, influenced also by the later work of the Austro-Marxists. Two particular aspects of industrial change as conceived by some Marxists, but in a more qualified way by Marx himself – the growing misery of the working class, linked with the increasing mechanization of production and rising unemployment, and the recurrent economic crises which would culminate in some kind of 'breakdown' of capitalism – were also discussed by Schumpeter (pp. 34–42), and they constitute, as will be seen, a significant part of the context in which he developed his own very different conception of the decline of the capitalist social order.

Finally, Schumpeter looked at the Marxist synthesis as a whole, in which 'sociology and economics pervade each other' (p. 45) and examined in particular two central issues: the theory of imperialism and the theory of the 'self-destruction of capitalism'. On the first, he was mainly concerned to criticize the conceptions of Hilferding and Bauer, and to question the connection they had asserted between the development of trustified capitalism, protectionism and imperialist expansion; and he was indeed much more critical than he had been in his earlier essay (1919), also introducing into his discussion an apparent reference (p. 53) to the concept of 'social imperialism' that he had cited with approval in 1939. But his own variable conception of imperialism had many weaknesses and was never expounded in a systematic form after 1919 (see above, pages 45–50), with the consequence that his critical comments also have a fragmentary and inconclusive character, and some of the questions that they raise will be considered in a wider context later (see Chapter 8 below).

On the second issue, Schumpeter argued that there would be no purely economic breakdown of capitalism, and that a socialist order would not be realized 'automatically' (pp. 56–7). But on both these points he was largely in agreement not only with Hilferding, who insisted that 'the collapse of capitalism will be political and social, not economic; for the idea of a purely economic collapse makes no sense' (1910, p. 366), but also with Marx, who in the very passage that Schumpeter had cited (pp. 37–8) made the demise of capitalism and the transition to socialism dependent on 'the revolt of the working class' as well as on 'the centralization of the means of production and socialization of labour'. It is true that a major question then arises as to the relative importance of, and the interconnections between, these economic, social and political trends, and that Marx's discussion of the causes and consequences of economic crises was incomplete, thus giving rise to diverse later interpretations (Bottomore 1985, pp. 11–14), but the same problem confronts Schumpeter's alternative explanation of the transition from capitalism to socialism.

This alternative indeed still draws substantially upon Marxist thought, and in a broad sense it may be said that Schumpeter's precursory exposition of Marxism provides the background against which the argument of the rest of his book is constructed. First, he reasserted strongly – in complete agreement with Marx – that capitalism is 'by nature a form or method of economic change [which] not only never is but never can be stationary', and it 'incessantly revolutionizes the economic structure *from within*', in a process of 'creative destruction'; but these upheavals occur in 'discrete rushes', and the process of revolution and absorption of the results of revolution constitutes the business cycle (pp. 82–3). A salient feature in the development of twentieth-century capitalism to which Schumpeter devoted much of his analysis, having already referred to it more briefly in several earlier writings, was the growth and increasing dominance in the economy of large corporations, a phenomenon to which Hilferding had attributed major importance in his study of finance capital (1910) and in subsequent writings of the 1920s on 'organized capitalism'. Schumpeter concluded his own discussion of the role of large enterprises, and of the effects of oligopolistic or monopolistic practices, by saying that these large units should not be regarded as a 'necessary evil' but had in fact become 'the most powerful engine' of economic progress, and 'in particular of the long-run expansion of total output'. Hence, 'in this respect, perfect competition is not only impossible but inferior, and has no title to being set up as a model of ideal efficiency'. And his final comment (a salutary thought for the present time!) was that 'socialists should rely for their criticisms on the virtues of a socialist economy rather than on those of the competitive model' (p. 106).

Rather surprisingly, however, Schumpeter now paid scant attention to the role of the banks in capitalist development, although in earlier writings he had attributed great importance to it, and in an article published a few years later (1946b) still defined capitalism as follows:

> a society which entrusts its economic progress to the guidance of the private businessman. This may be said to imply, first, private ownership of nonpersonal means of production, such as land, mines, industrial plant and equipment; and, second, production for private profit. But, third, the institution of bank credit is so essential to the functioning of the capitalist system that, though not strictly implied in the definition, it should be added to the other two criteria. (p. 184)

This is a somewhat inadequate definition,[4] and in particular, with regard to the role of banks (and more recently of other large financial institutions), too restrictive. A recent author (Swoboda 1984, p. 19) has observed that 'Schumpeter's conception of the financing of firms can be characterized by neglecting equity financing, stressing financing by retained earnings and overemphasizing credit financing', and he cites the conclusion reached by Streissler (1982) that 'if Schumpeter's theory was influenced by observations from the Austrian situation before the First World War he must have misinterpreted the data', for 'equity financing was quite the rule [and] banks either became partners of successful firms or placed their shares on the stock exchange'.

Hilferding's conception of finance capital as a distinct stage in the development of capitalism, involving a close integration of financial (bank) capital with industrial capital, thus seems closer to the real situation, at least in the case of Austria and Germany, and probably more widely,[5] than does Schumpeter's more limited view of the role of bank credit; and it provided a schema within which the process of 'trustification', or the 'socialization' of the economy, could be more systematically analysed. Schumpeter himself used the Marxist concept of 'socialization' from an early date, and notably in his article (1920/21) on the possibility of socialism, where he defined socialization as the 'sustaining idea' of the socialist movement, encompassing both a gradual historical process and conscious political action aiming at its full realization (see above, pages 36–7). He continued to refer to socialization in subsequent writings, but did not examine in any systematic way the nature of this historical process and its possible outcomes, and in particular largely ignored that part of Hilferding's later conception of 'organized capitalism' (a term also used occasionally by Schumpeter) which emphasized the extension of economic planning and the increasing involvement of the state in the regulation of economic life (Bottomore 1991b; entry on 'organized capitalism', p. 404).

From Schumpeter's standpoint the process of socialization meant above all the increasing dominance of large bureaucratic organizations and a continuous process of rationalization in the capitalist economy, leading to the 'obsolescence of the entrepreneurial function'. The entrepreneur is the agent of innovation – introducing new technology, opening up new sources of supply and new markets, carrying out industrial reorganization – but 'this social function is already losing importance and is bound to lose it at an accelerating rate in the future', for 'innovation itself is being reduced to routine [and] technological progress is increasingly becoming the business of teams of trained specialists . . . Thus, economic progress tends to become depersonalized and automatized. Bureau and committee work tends to replace individual action' (pp. 132–3). This thesis has attracted a great deal of criticism in recent years, much of it concentrating on the fact that 'there has been more room for dynamic entrepreneurial activity than Schumpeter foresaw, especially in smaller scale operations' (Heertje 1981, p. x). But this is by no means the major criticism that can be made. In the half-century that has passed since

Schumpeter wrote his book there has been massive innovation – in technology, markets, the organization of industry – or, expressed more generally, a great expansion and development of capitalism as a world system, and this has been predominantly the work of large corporations which Schumpeter himself described as innovators in an earlier study (see above, page 73). So the entrepreneurial function has *not* disappeared, but has simply changed its form, and we can see in the conduct of modern corporations, including publicly owned corporations, a mixture of functions (to some extent existing in embryo in smaller enterprises) ranging from more or less routine management and the contributions of various kinds of trained specialists, to entrepreneurship; the latter being performed collectively by boards of directors and other managers, though particular individuals may still have a distinctive role. In short, both the structure of a corporation, and the entrepreneurial, innovative function, are far more complex than Schumpeter's simplistic model suggested.

From the thesis of the vanishing entrepreneur Schumpeter went on to consider the implications for the social situation of the bourgeoisie as a whole. Entrepreneurs, he argued, are the most active part of this class, and 'economically and sociologically, directly and indirectly, the bourgeoisie therefore depends on the entrepreneur and, as a class, lives and will die with him'. And he summed up his argument by saying that

> since capitalist enterprise, by its very achievements, tends to automatize progress, we conclude that it tends to make itself superfluous – to break to pieces under the pressure of its own success. The perfectly bureaucratized giant industrial unit not only ousts the small or medium-sized firm and 'expropriates' its owner, but in the end it also ousts the entrepreneur and expropriates the bourgeoisie as a class which in the process stands to lose not only its income but also what is infinitely more important, its function. (p. 134)

Two other factors, according to Schumpeter, contributed to the decline of the bourgeoisie. The 'destruction of the protecting strata', above all the aristocracy which performed, on behalf of the bourgeoisie and in an active symbiosis with it, the functions of managing the state and ruling society, left the bourgeoisie 'politically helpless and unable not only to lead its nation but even to take care of its particular class interest' (pp. 136–8). More generally, the growth of large enterprises destroys the 'institutional framework' of capitalist society by eliminating many small producers and traders, and by

> pushing into the background all those institutions, the institutions of property [i.e. individual ownership] and free contracting in particular, that expressed the needs and ways of the truly 'private' economic activity. . . . The capitalist process, by substituting a mere parcel of shares for the walls of and the machines in a factory, takes the life out of the idea of property. (pp. 141–2)

On both these points, however, Schumpeter was quite simply wrong, led astray perhaps by a dual nostalgia for an idealized heroic age of capitalism with the rugged individualist as its central figure, and for the social and political institutions of the vanished Habsburg monarchy. At all events, contrary to his expectations and predictions, the bourgeoisie, over the past half-century, has shown itself to be quite capable of ruling the nation; and share ownership, as a major form of private wealth, is very far from having drained the life out of the idea of property.

Schumpeter's analysis as a whole does conform closely in one respect with the scheme which he outlined in his general study of classes (1927b; see above, pages 51–4), in dealing exclusively with the 'fall' of a class through the loss of its social function, while ignoring the 'rise' of a new class. Here, as elsewhere, he paid very little attention to the class structure as such, although in one or two of his writings he did make brief reference to the 'new middle class', the peasantry, and industrial workers (e.g. 1929; see above, pages 55–6). But the social category, other than the entrepreneur, which engaged his main interest, was the stratum of intellectuals, whose contribution to the decline of capitalism he greatly exaggerated. Capitalism, he argued, 'unlike any other type of society . . . inevitably and by virtue of the very logic of its civilization creates, educates and subsidizes a vested interest in social unrest' (p. 146), and after discussing such issues of the 1930s as 'intellectual unemployment' which produced, according to him, large numbers of discontented and resentful individuals, he claimed that intellectuals had invaded the labour movement, radicalizing it and 'imparting a revolutionary bias to the most bourgeois trade-union practices', so that although they did not create the labour movement they turned it into something quite different from what it would be without them (pp. 153–4). Evidently, Schumpeter had no great love for intellectuals in general, and his strong feelings on the subject led him into passionate denunciation rather than scholarly enquiry. A more serious sociology of intellectuals would have to recognize that this is a social category with indefinite boundaries (as Schumpeter conceded), extremely heterogeneous, and characterized historically by very diverse and fluctuating political attitudes, which in any case are never uniform but range from indifference to extremes of conservatism or left-wing radicalism. Even in those periods when left-wing social thought seems to have a certain pre-eminence, as Schumpeter may have considered was the case in the 1930s (and others again in the 1960s), it would be difficult to show that a substantial minority, let alone majority, of intellectuals actually held or expressed radical views.

A second issue concerns the nature and extent of the influence that intellectuals exercise, whatever their social and political opinions may be. Schumpeter attributed to them an autonomous and powerful influence, but this seems doubtful, for it can just as well be asserted, with rather more empirical evidence in support, that the diverse politics of intellectuals are determined mainly by the direction of their 'ties with society's fundamental classes and groups' (Brym 1980, p. 71). So it is not intellectuals who radicalize the labour movement (or other social movements) but social movements which, in particular circumstances, radicalize some intellectuals. There may be, as social movements develop, a reciprocal influence, but in general it seems probable, contrary to Schumpeter's opinion, that in most places and at most times, intellectuals as a whole have a comparatively slight impact upon the course of social and political life, though the ideas of a few exceptional thinkers (Marx, Darwin or Einstein) may in the longer term, and in very different ways, have a more profound effect.

Schumpeter's observations on the role of intellectuals formed part of a more general discussion of what he saw as a continuing process of erosion of capitalist values. He argued that capitalism

> creates a critical frame of mind which, after having destroyed the moral authority of so many other institutions, in the end turns against its own; the bourgeois finds to his amazement that the rationalist attitude does not stop at the credentials of kings and

popes but goes on to attack private property and the whole scheme of bourgeois values. The bourgeois fortress becomes politically defenceless. (p. 143)

But he devoted only one or two pages of quite inadequate analysis to this phenomenon, in which he was mainly concerned to reinterpret rational criticism as a 'rationalization' of underlying sentiments or impulses, in the manner of Pareto (p. 143, n. 1; pp. 144–5); and the principal unanswered question to be examined here is how far bourgeois values or the bourgeois 'ideology' – that is to say, the body of ideas in which the values and aspirations of a social class, or other major social group, are formulated in a more or less coherent and systematic way – have in fact been eroded in the way that Schumpeter suggested.

The principal components of bourgeois ideology, I would suggest, are the ideas of private property, individualism (and as a pre-eminent aspect of it, personal achievement, especially in the economic field and measured largely by a monetary standard), and the nation.[6] When Schumpeter argued that corporate ownership 'takes the life out of private property' he was not (whatever he may have thought) pointing to an established fact, but possibly to a tendency, and certainly to a body of criticism, emanating from social movements and individual thinkers, which was directed against individualistic conceptions of property and has been concisely summarized as the view that in an advanced industrial society property rights have to be defined as 'social rights which determine the relations of the various groups of owners and non-owners to the system of production, and prescribe what each group's share of the social product shall be' (Schlatter 1951, p. 273). In the fifty years since Schumpeter was writing there has been a further expansion (greater indeed than in the period with which he was familiar) of social or collective property, in the form both of public ownership and of ever larger, now increasingly multinational, corporations, as well as a significant growth of social rights in welfare states (Marshall 1950). But there is no evidence that shareholding, as distinct from direct ownership of physical plant, has attenuated the sense of private property, and those who run the large corporations as directors and executives are very much aware of being engaged in the productive use of private property, a part of which they usually 'own' in a legal sense, while they collectively 'possess' the whole of it in the sense that they effectively control the process of production and the disposition of the product.[7] Furthermore, a substantial part of production is still carried on by businesses (including large ones) in which the capital is owned directly by an individual, a family or a partnership (Bottomore and Brym 1989). On the other side, the actual extension of social rights into the sphere of ownership of productive property has been very limited, and there has been continuous criticism, from the standpoint of bourgeois values, of the alleged inefficiency and excessively bureaucratic organization of publicly owned enterprises. During the 1980s public ownership was indeed directly attacked in many capitalist countries through extensive programmes of privatization, and this revival of private ownership as a fact and an ideology was given a further impetus by the collapse of the communist regimes in Eastern Europe at the end of the decade. Far from becoming increasingly debilitated, therefore, private property in the sphere of production appears to have maintained and even increased its vitality, though we should not necessarily conclude that this trend will continue in the medium- or long-term future.

Individualism, in the bourgeois scheme of values, has always been closely associated with the idea of private property, but confusion exists between private property as individual ownership of means of production and 'personal' property involving such things as house ownership and the possession of some stock, whether small or large, of wealth.[8] As Mills (1951, p. 34) observed with respect to American society, economic independence as a producer was a fundamental element in the individualist doctrine and had some reality in the small-propertied world of the early nineteenth century, but was no more than an 'ideological figment' in the twentieth century when most Americans had become 'hired employees'. To this extent bourgeois individualism had been at least potentially undermined, as Schumpeter supposed, by the growth of large corporations, but the ideology has persisted, remaining powerful and influential in all capitalist countries, even though challenged by alternative conceptions emphasizing the degree to which individual rights and liberties are gained and secured by collective action. One factor that helps to sustain the bourgeois conception is probably a widespread apprehension – enhanced by the experience of totalitarian regimes – about the increasing power of the state and invasion of privacy (though this is by no means due only to the activities of the state), and a more diffuse sense of living in 'over-regulated' societies; issues which will be examined further in discussing Schumpeter's ideas about a possible transition to socialism and the nature of a socialist system.

The third major element in the bourgeois scheme of values is the idea of the nation as a focus of primary loyalties, which plays an important role both positively in fostering a sense of unity and an attachment to 'traditional' values, and negatively in countering the divisiveness implied by the ideas of class polarization and class conflict. But Schumpeter – unlike Weber, and, among the Austro-Marxists, Bauer and Renner – gave little attention to this subject, rather surprisingly if we consider his experience of the rise of nationalist movements in the Habsburg Empire, although he approached some aspects of it in his study of imperialism, particularly in his references to 'social imperialism' (see above, pages 48–9). At all events, nationalism, and its development in some periods and in various forms as imperialist expansion, has remained one of the mainstays of bourgeois thought, by contrast with the internationalism expressed in most versions of socialist thought; and it has demonstrated throughout the twentieth century, up to the most recent times, its powerful influence on political practice.

One important reason for Schumpeter's neglect of nationalism is to be found in his general approach to the decline of bourgeois values, which is treated as an immanent process, quite unrelated to the emergence of alternative values expressed in the ideology of another class. Indeed, his whole analysis of the decline of capitalism takes this form. The underlying cause is the progressive 'socialization' of the economy, resulting in the dominance of large corporations, a phenomenon which Schumpeter did not attempt to explain but treated as a given empirical fact while seeming indeed to accept a broadly Marxist view of its causes. Its principal consequence is the elimination of the entrepreneur – tacitly conceived for the most part as an individual person although there are occasional references, which vitiate the whole argument, suggesting the possible existence of 'collective entrepreneurs' – and with that an increasing debility of the whole bourgeois class, whose essential values of private property and invidualism are gradually eroded. This erosion, determined in the first place by economic evolution, is then accelerated by the criticisms of capitalist society emanating from, so to speak, 'free-floating' intellectuals.

The main thesis which Schumpeter's analysis was intended to establish, as stated in his prologue to Part II, is that the capitalist system will not break down 'under the weight of economic failure, but that its very success undermines the social institutions which protect it, and "inevitably" creates conditions in which it will not be able to live' (p. 61). This success – the massive development of productive forces and the consequent increase in total output – is conceived in terms which do not differ greatly from those used by Marx and later Marxists to describe the revolutionary achievements of capitalism as a mode of production; and in the continuation of his argument Schumpeter also remained close to Marxism in his account of the gradual socialization of the economy which prepared the way for socialism. Where he diverged was in paying little attention to the elements of failure within the successful advance of the capitalist economy – extremes of wealth and poverty, unemployment, the effects of economic crises. Beginning to write his book in the 1930s, soon after the great depression, he did not consider how far that experience itself contributed to an erosion of capitalist values, and on the other side to a strengthening of socialist values in the working-class movement. The depression was not a total 'breakdown' of the capitalist economy, such that a socialist economy would necessarily and automatically emerge from it (an idea which, as we have seen, was dismissed by many Marxist thinkers), but it *was* a severe partial breakdown which had major consequences for the balance of power between classes, and in due course for the post-war development of capitalism.

But Schumpeter also deliberately excluded from his analysis the idea of an opposition between classes, arguing in his critique of Marx that

> the exaggeration of the definiteness and importance of the dividing line between the capitalist class . . . and the proletariat was surpassed only by the exaggeration of the antagonism between them . . . [whereas] it should be obvious that their relation is, in normal times, primarily one of cooperation and that any theory to the contrary must draw largely on pathological cases for verification. (p. 19)

Disregarding, for the moment, the inaccuracy of this statement we should note that in taking such a view Schumpeter made the decline of capitalism truly a process of *self*-destruction in which no alternative 'rising' class played a part, and hence left indeterminate the nature of any post-capitalist system. And just as in his analysis of this decline there are erroneous, ambiguous and contradictory judgements – entrepreneurship and innovation did not disappear (far from it) and sometimes he recognized this fact; the idea of private property did not wither away; competition, after being dismissed as an 'inferior' engine of economic progress, was then treated as a continuing element of capitalist dynamism – so too, as we shall see, is Schumpeter's account of socialism as a likely 'heir apparent' replete with ambiguities and misconceptions.

Notes

1. In the following text, while the original date of publication is cited, page references are given to the 1987 edition, which includes as an appendix Schumpeter's prefaces to the first three editions and his last article (1950) on 'the march into socialism'.
2. In the conclusion to Part II (1942, p. 163) he noted that the decline of capitalism had not yet proceeded so far in any country as to make possible any confident assertion about how far it would go.

   > Industrial integration is far from being complete. Competition, actual and potential, is still a major factor in any business situation. Enterprise is still active, the leadership of the bourgeois group still the prime mover of the economic process. The middle class is still an economic power. Bourgeois standards and bourgois motivations . . . are still alive. Survival of traditions – and family ownership of controlling parcels of stock – still make many an executive behave as the owner-manager did of old. The bourgeois family has not yet died.

   And in his article of 1950 Schumpeter presented a revised version of his thesis: 'the capitalist order tends to destroy itself and . . . centralist socialism is . . . a likely heir apparent', although the 'observable tendencies may be compatible with more than one outcome' or 'may "stick" at some halfway house' (1942, pp. 422–3).
3. This idea had been expounded more fully in Schumpeter's (1919) original formulation of his 'atavistic' theory of imperialism (see above, pages 46–7).
4. Especially in excluding the phenomenon of wage labour, which in

Marxist economic thought is conceived as the transformation of labour power itself into a commodity. A more adequate definition was provided by Max Weber (1923, pp. 207–9) who, after emphasizing as a basic defining characteristic 'the method of enterprise', listed six presuppositions or conditions for the existence of modern capitalism: (i) rational capital accounting, involving, 'the appropriation of all physical means of production . . . as disposable property of autonomous private industrial enterprises; (ii) freedom of the market; (iii) rational technology, 'which implies mechanization'; (iv) calculable law; (v) free labour, i.e. the presence of persons 'who are not only legally in the position, but are also economically compelled, to sell their labour on the market without restriction'; and (vi) the commercialization of economic life, by which is meant 'the general use of commercial instruments to represent share rights in enterprise, and also in property ownership'.

5. See Bottomore (1981, pp. 6–7). Nevertheless, Hilferding's conception itself raises a number of problems; see Harris (1991).
6. I examined these components more fully in a previous study (Bottomore 1981, pp. 32–6) and in the following text I shall only summarize briefly the main points.
7. On the various distinctions which need to be made in considering the sociological meaning of 'property', see Hegedüs (1976) and also the interpretation of the individualist theories by Macpherson (1962).
8. For a broader discussion which brings out the diverse meanings of individualism, see Lukes (1973), who begins by observing that it 'is a word that has come to be used with an unusual lack of precision' (p. ix).

CHAPTER 7

SOCIALISM AND DEMOCRACY

Schumpeter defined socialism in a very restrictive way (p. 167) as:

> an institutional pattern in which the control over means of production and over production itself is vested with a central authority – or, as we may say, in which, as a matter of principle, the economic affairs of society belong to the public and not to the private sphere

and he explicitly excluded from his analysis many other social and cultural aspects, concluding, after some absurd comments on the professed ideals of socialists, that the doctrine was so 'culturally indeterminate' as not to be accessible to reasonable discussion (p. 170). This narrow approach had several important consequences. First, his concentration on the nature of socialism as an economic system involved treating the transition from capitalism to socialism as an almost purely economic process, and the key concept in his argument, borrowed from Marxism, was that of 'socialization'. As he wrote:

> Most of the argument of Part II may be summed up in the Marxian proposition that the economic process tends to socialize *itself* – and also the human soul. By this we mean that the technological, organizational, commercial, administrative and psychological prerequisites of socialism tend to be fulfilled more and more. (p. 219)

True, he also observed that while the capitalist process 'shapes things and souls for socialism', the transition 'will still require distinct action and still present a number of problems' (p. 220); but he paid little attention to the nature, or the sources, of this 'distinct action', and the general impression conveyed by his analysis is that of an economic mechanism which is remorselessly grinding out a socialist future.

Hence in this respect Schumpeter also appears as much more of an economic determinist than do the followers of Marx, who conceived socialism as resulting from the conscious actions of a class, though not all of them paid serious attention to the complexities and difficulties of class action, or to the problematic relationship between a class, the party or parties claiming to represent its interests, and the party leadership.[1] Schumpeter's view derived from his rejection of the notion of a fundamental opposition between classes in capitalist society, so that the decline of capitalism had to be represented almost exclusively as a necessary consequence of that process of economic development which eliminates the entrepreneur and the attachment to private property; and it remains unclear why socialism, in any sense which can be elicited from its reality as a historical movement, should in fact be seen as the most likely successor. As one recent commentator (Fellner 1981, p. 61) has suggested, capitalism might reasonably

> be expected to include a succession of systems rather than to be a single system . . . [and] whether . . . Schumpeter has explained the transformation of a system in this sense into another variety of capitalism or, as he believed, a decomposition process leading into centralized socialism, is a question which his reasoning does not decide.

From such a standpoint one might argue that two separate (but closely related, since both depend in part upon the 'socialization' of the economy) processes of development were occurring in twentieth-century capitalism: (i) a movement towards socialism which Schumpeter tried to explain in a one-sided fashion, inadequately, and sometimes contradicting himself, by the disappearance of the entrepreneur, without setting this in the general context of class structure and class relations or paying any attention to the socio-political role of the working class; and (ii) a movement towards a new type of capitalist system, which Hilferding had described as 'organized capitalism'. Schumpeter occasionally used this term, but only very belatedly did he introduce into his analysis one of the principal elements in Hilferding's conception, namely the increasing involvement of the state in the management of the economy. The greater part of Schumpeter's discussion is devoted to the question of whether socialism 'can work' and to problems of the transition (Chapters 16–19). It is noteworthy, first, for a defence of the possibility of rational economic calculation in a centrally planned socialist society against such criticisms as those of Mises;[2] secondly, for an analysis of the comparative efficiency of capitalist and socialist economies in which he argued that 'the planning of progress . . . would be incomparably more effective' in eliminating cyclical ups and downs 'than any automatic or manipulative variations of the rate of interest or the supply of credit can be', concluding (pp. 195–6) that the whole of the argument

> might be put in a nutshell by saying that socialization means a stride beyond big business on the way that has been chalked out by it or, what amounts to the same thing, that socialist management may conceivably prove as superior to big-business capitalism as big-business capitalism has proved to be to the kind of competitive capitalism of which the English industry of a hundred years ago was the prototype

and thirdly, for a discussion of bureaucracy in which he argued that it is 'an inevitable complement to modern economic development' which will be 'more than ever essential in a socialist commonwealth' (p. 206), and while recognizing that bureaucratic methods may often have 'a depressing influence on the most active minds' (p. 207), considered that such problems might be at least partially overcome by various incentives, both social and economic.

Only later, in a chapter added in 1946, in his preface to the third edition and in his article of 1950, did Schumpeter begin to give more attention to the role of government, the actions of socialist parties (still not viewed as 'class parties', however) and the effects of two world wars, while also conceding the possibility that the process of socialization might come to a halt at some 'halfway house'. 'Many facts', he wrote (p. 377), 'go to show that, irrespective of the Russian element in the case, the effects of the Second World War on the social situation in Europe would have been similar to those of the First World War, only stronger. That is to say, we should have witnessed acceleration of the existing trend toward a socialist organization of production *in the sense defined in this book*'. But this was what the Austro-Marxists had been saying much earlier, and notably Renner (1916) in his discussion of the 'state penetration of the economy', advancing towards 'direct state management of the economy', in the First World War (see Bottomore and Goode 1978, p. 26); and it was a question which preoccupied many social scientists at that time – Schumpeter himself in his article of 1920/21, Hilferding in his account of the development of organized capitalism and Weber (1918a, pp. 331–2) who considered, however, that although 'a progressive elimination of private capitalism is no doubt theoretically conceivable' it would 'certainly not be the outcome of this war'.

It would be generally agreed that the Second World War did have a considerable influence on the movement towards socialism, by demonstrating the feasibility and effectiveness of national planning and more extensive state management of the economy when directed to a clearly conceived end. But this was only one of the major influences at work. Another was the greatly increased post-war strength of the European socialist parties (signalled initially by the sweeping electoral victory of the British Labour Party in 1945), and also of some communist parties – an accession of strength which was itself due to changes in the climate of political opinion. The victory over the fascist powers was widely seen as an opportunity to promote a more thoroughly democratic kind of society, particularly by extending the social rights of citizens,[3] and to ensure that the massive unemployment and poverty of the 1930s did not recur. As Postan (1967) argued, there had emerged from the pre-war political controversies a strong commitment to full employment that prevailed at least until the 1970s and had eventually developed into a broader doctrine and policy of economic growth, sponsored and managed in various ways by the state. In this sense the economic depression of the 1930s, although it did not lead to a 'breakdown' of capitalism, substantially weakened the capitalist order and was perhaps the most powerful factor bringing into existence a new type of 'welfare capitalism', characterized by some degree of 'mixed (public and private) economy', the allocation and distribution of a large part, between 40 per cent and 50 per cent, of the gross domestic product (GDP) by the state, and a more general state regulation of the economy, in many different forms, on a scale previously unknown except in wartime.

But there was yet a third powerful influence. The emergence of the USSR after the war as a major industrial and military power constituted, or in any case was perceived as, a serious threat to the capitalist order, all the more so when communist regimes were imposed upon other East European countries. The threat had two aspects: first, the promise held out of full employment, greater equality and planned, sustained economic development, all of which were capable of attracting support, and even emulation, if the West European societies appeared to be reverting to the conditions of the 1930s; but secondly, the consolidation and possible expansion of totalitarian regimes. The threat was countered primarily by the American Marshall Plan, which was a major factor in rebuilding the European economies in a predominantly capitalist form, and was widely supported because it was seen at the same time as aiding the re-establishment of democratic political systems, in sharp contrast with the East European countries, which remained Stalinist, governed by repression and terror, until 1953, and continued thereafter as authoritarian one-party regimes. But the capitalism which was re-established in Western Europe differed greatly from the pre-war type, as a result of the internal social changes that I have indicated (and the Marshall Plan itself facilitated, or even made necessary in some respects, an extension of economic planning); and it was successful over the next two decades precisely because of this difference.

Schumpeter paid heed to some of these post-war changes in his discussion of the economic policies implemented during the first two years of the Labour government in Britain (preface to third edition, pp. 415–20), and in his article of 1950 (pp. 421–31), emphasizing those which strengthened the movement towards socialism. The situation in Britain, he considered, was 'proof that the ethos of capitalism is gone' (p. 416), a judgement which reads very strangely in the 1990s. More generally, he summarized his reasons for continuing to believe 'that the capitalist order tends to destroy itself' (pp. 423–4), noting the extent to which the implications of this process of disintegration of capitalist society were being accepted by the business class itself and by large numbers of economists opposed in principle to socialism (p. 424); and he also pointed to the 'accelerating' effects of the world economic crisis of the 1930s and the Second World War (p. 426), though he did not stay to analyse the nature of those effects. In his final article Schumpeter also made some concessions: the 'observable tendencies' might not work themselves out fully, or they might be compatible with several different outcomes, but he did not in fact rate these possibilities very highly (p. 423) and reasserted his view that the 'long-run contours of social history . . . are a matter of much deeper forces . . . of more fundamental tendencies' (p. 427). Hence he never took very seriously the idea that capitalism in its pre-war form might be transformed into a different kind of economy and social order – perhaps corresponding in some way with his unexplained conception of a 'halfway house' – which would nevertheless remain distinctively capitalist. And the principal reason why he did not pursue this line of thought is that he failed to envisage a situation in which the capitalist class (or the 'business class' as he more loosely called it) would succeed in adapting itself to the post-war conditions and in launching a counter-offensive against socialism.

Underlying this failure was Schumpeter's whole mistaken conception of the decline of capitalism. The innovator, or 'entrepreneur', instead of disappearing, acquired a new lease of life as a 'collective subject' in the increasingly powerful and highly innovative large corporations, but also as an individual in small and medium-sized businesses for which rapid and sustained economic growth provided fresh opportunities, especially in the expanding services sector of the economy. So also the capitalist class as a whole became stronger rather than weaker, its strength enhanced by the growth of the middle class and the contraction of the working class, while at the same time the social and political attitudes of all classes were affected by increasing prosperity and the expectation of steady economic growth and rising standards of living in what came to be seen as a relatively stable economy and social order. On the other side, the economic, political and cultural situation in the Soviet-type societies of Eastern Europe, which claimed to represent 'real socialism', had an inhibiting influence – no matter how vigorously this model was rejected by Western socialists – on any further movement towards socialism in the capitalist countries.[4] Schumpeter's analysis went astray principally because he adhered too closely to the unrealistic notion of the vanishing entrepreneur, did not take account of the changes in class structure, the shift of economic activity towards the services sector or the remoter consequences of the expanding economic role of government; but he also neglected the influence of the 'lead' country – a role performed for three decades after the war by the USA – in the overall process of capitalist development.[5]

Today, of course, we have the advantage of being able to look back over a period of exceptionally rapid development, during which time the tendencies I have outlined above have become much clearer, and we can also observe, and try to analyse the implications of, the collapse of the countries of 'real socialism'. Nevertheless, even in the 1940s it would have been possible, in a work that was intended to delineate the main tendencies of capitalist development over a medium-term future of several decades, to consider a wider range of questions than Schumpeter actually concerned himself with, and the relative narrowness of his approach will be shown again in the next chapter, in a comparison between different theoretical models for the analysis of twentieth-century capitalism.

One major section of Schumpeter's study (Part IV) was concerned with the relation between democracy and socialism, and here, as we shall see, he defined his subject matter in the same restrictive fashion as he had done in his account of socialism itself. First, however, he commented on the democratic credentials, in a broad sense, of socialist parties, with a brief reference to the idea of the 'dictatorship of the proletariat' and to the actual dictatorship in the USSR, and then continued with a highly tendentious account of the record of West European socialist parties, in which he managed, among other things, to avoid any mention of their long-continued and eventually successful campaigns for universal adult suffrage, which is one of the principal foundations of late twentieth-century democracy. His own preliminary definition ran as follows: 'democracy is a policitcal *method*, that is to say, a certain type of institutional arrangement for arriving at political – legislative and administrative – decisions and hence incapable of being an end in itself' (p. 242), and after a critical review of what he called the 'classical doctrine' he then completed the definition by saying that it is a method through which 'individuals acquire the power to decide by means of a competitive struggle for the people's vote' (p. 269). It seems evident that this conception, not only in general but in some of its details, was derived mainly from the work of Max Weber (though there is no acknowledgement of any such indebtedness),[6] but it was also doubtless influenced by the cognate 'élite theory' of Pareto.[7]

The salient feature in Schumpeter's discussion of democracy is the analogy he suggested between the political process and the market economy. Democracy is conceived as an institutional arrangement in which various groups and individuals – equivalent to businesses and entrepreneurs – compete for the votes of electors, who are the political 'consumers'; and the analogy is emphasized by his quotation of a politician's comment to the effect that 'What businessmen do not understand is that exactly as they are dealing in oil so I am dealing in votes' (p. 285). This is, despite Schumpeter's protestations to the contrary (p. 285, n. 3), not only a very partial view, but also cynical and tending to debase the idea of democracy, and while not being totally unreal in an age of massive party expenditure on public relations and political circuses it is nevertheless a travesty of the historical development of the democratic movement. In fact Schumpeter himself, in referring to a historical association – or even a possible causal connection – between the emergence of capitalism and the growth of modern democracy, introduced such notions as rational action, individual responsibility, self-discipline, tolerance and equality, which seem to belong rather to the classical doctrine.[8] As a whole, his exposition of the 'alternative theory' is confused and vacillating, making all kinds of concessions along the way, and in particular it does not exemplify a rigorous use of that historical method to which, in his later methodological writings, he attributed such great importance. The actual history of the democratic movement, like that of the socialist movement, is largely ignored, and the historical narratives and reflections which appear at various points throughout the book are purely descriptive, even anecdotal, rather than being related to a theoretical model from which explanatory propositions about the development of modern capitalism as a social order might be derived.

Schumpeter wrote only briefly on the prospects for democracy in a socialist society. Referring to the discussions in the German Commission on Socialization in 1919 he noted the opposition to the workers' councils, and more generally to the ideas of industrial or economic democracy which, he claimed, had little precise meaning and would not play any significant part in a socialist regime, largely because many of the interests that this kind of democracy was intended to protect would have ceased to exist (p. 300).[9] But democracy in his sense – with general elections, parties and parliaments – could perfectly well exist in a socialist society, on the assumption that the society itself had attained a condition of 'maturity', including particularly 'the ability to establish the socialist order in a democratic way and the existence of a bureaucracy of adequate standing and experience' (p. 301). In addition, socialism achieved in these circumstances would also 'command an advantage of possibly decisive importance', namely that internal conflict would be likely to diminish as a result of more general agreement on the fundamentals of the institutional structure, and even though some distinct economic interests or conflicts would remain, and there would be non-economic issues to disagree about, 'a good case may be made out for expecting that the sum total of controversial matter would be decreased' (pp. 301–2).

On the other hand, the possibility existed that there would be deviations from this democratic model, and 'even if [on the assumption of economic maturity] there is no necessity for sweating the people by means of a Gosplan, the task of keeping the democratic course may prove to be extremely delicate' because of the 'tremendous power over the people inherent in the socialist organization. After all, effective management of the socialist economy means dictatorship not *of* but *over* the proletariat in the factory' (p. 302), or as Weber (1918b) had said, a dictatorship of the official rather than of the proletariat. Much of Schumpeter's discussion here, including his comments on some of the problems that socialist democracy might face, does not diverge greatly from the views held by the Austro-Marxists, particularly as they were expressed by Bauer (1919, and other writings; see Bottomore and Goode, 1978, Introduction pp. 26–7) in his conception of the 'slow revolution', and in the later analyses by Hilferding (1940, 1941) of the increasing power of the modern nation-state and the conditions in which totalitarian regimes could emerge. The major difference, and an important one, is that the Austro-Marxists continued to emphasize the importance of economic democracy – that is, some degree of workers' participation in, and control over, the management of enterprises – both as a constraint on the power of the state and its agencies, and as a means of self-education in the practice of democratic citizenship. But there is one final curiosity in Schumpeter's discussion: namely, his concluding observation that if the possible deviations from a democratic system actually took place then socialism would mean 'no closer approximation to the ideals enshrined in the classical doctrine' (p. 302). So it appears that this rejected 'classical doctrine' is, after all, a kind of touchstone by which to judge whether a social order is more, or less, democratic, and the confusion is complete.

The issues which Schumpeter raised, in a highly provocative manner, concerning the development and decline of capitalism, the emergence of socialism as its possible successor, and the relation of these tendencies to the idea and practice of democracy, are of fundamental importance to economic sociology, as indeed to any worthwhile sociology at all. His theoretical models, methodological choices and explanatory propositions, which I have examined critically here and in the preceding chapters, locating them so far as is possible in their intellectual and social context, should now therefore be considered in more general terms from the standpoint of the scope of economic sociology as it can be conceived today. What is, in fact, Schumpeter's usable legacy? To answer this question we need to compare his work with that of other thinkers, most eminent among them Marx and Weber, who constructed divergent models, possessed a different 'vision'; and beyond this to consider how far some more recent studies, in a period of continuing and accelerating change, have brought a new understanding and/or provoked new questions.

Notes

1. One major issue in this relationship was examined by Michels (1911), and other aspects were discussed by Adler (1933) and Hilferding (1941), while more recently numerous critical studies have been devoted to the phenomenon of one-party dictatorships in the former communist regimes of Eastern Europe.
2. Schumpeter (p. 173) based his case largely on the work of Barone (1908), and referred also to the later work of Lange and Taylor (1938) and others (see above, page 57). I have discussed the 'socialist calculation debate', including its more recent forms, in Bottomore (1990, ch. 4).
3. See especially T. H. Marshall (1950) whose work expressed very clearly a broadly accepted view of the needs of post-war reconstruction.
4. I have discussed some of these issues more fully elsewhere (Bottomore 1975, 1984, 1991a).

5. In particular, Maddison (1982, p. 79) saw as a major defect in Schumpeter's analysis of long waves his failure to distinguish between the 'lead' country and others, and in a later study also his neglect of the role of government (1991, p. 103). Such criticisms can obviously be directed more widely against Schumpeter's whole theory of the later stages of capitalist development.
6. The two principal texts in which Weber's idea of democracy was formulated are 'Politics as a vocation' (1919) and *Economy and Society*, Part I, Chapter 3 (1921).
7. In discussing 'human nature in politics' Schumpeter (p. 256) referred briefly to Pareto's contribution to a growing recognition of the 'extra-rational and irrational' elements in human behaviour, and in a later article (1949, p. 141) he praised especially Pareto's 'fundamental principle that what individuals, groups, and nations actually do must find its explanation in something much deeper than the creeds and slogans that are used in order to verbalize action'.
8. One major aspect of this growth of democracy, to which Schumpeter paid no attention, is the gradual extension of citizenship, analysed in the classic study by T. H. Marshall (1950).
9. This differs markedly from the view expressed in his article of 1920/21, where he argued that the advent of a socialist economy would necessarily be accompanied by changes in the political system, from an exclusively parliamentary democracy to a 'council democracy' (see above, pages 37–8). The change in his outlook can be attributed partly no doubt to changes in the intellectual and political climate over the intervening twenty years, but this may also have coloured his interpretation, in 1942, of the debates which actually took place in the Commission on Socialization.

CHAPTER 8

THE REALM OF ECONOMIC SOCIOLOGY

Economic sociology is not simply a specialized field of study, akin to other specialisms within general sociology; it has also been the principal foundation on which several major social theories have been built. This is most obviously the case with Marx's 'economic interpretation of history' – more generally known as 'historical materialism' or 'the materialist conception of history', though these terms are misleading in some respects[1] – which asserts that the ultimate cause and principal motive force of all important historical events is to be found in the economic development of society;[2] that is to say, in changes in the mode of production. The different modes of production, according to Marx's conception, distinguish the principal stages in the history of human society and are constituted by two factors: the 'forces of production' (in broad terms, the level of technology) and the 'relations of production' (that is, the relations between social groups which are engaged in different ways in the process of production, and especially the relations between the two principal classes of those who 'own' and manage the system of production, and the 'direct producers' who contribute their labour). But in Marxist analyses of the ways in which major social changes are actually brought about very diverse approaches and interpretations have been possible, depending partly upon whether greater emphasis is placed upon the progress of technology (which suggests an underlying technological determinism) or upon the relations, and particularly the conflicts, between classes; and more generally upon how the interconnection between these two factors is conceived. A further problem

The realm of economic sociology 113

arises in considering the nature of the connection between the mode of production, or economic 'base', and a 'superstructure' which includes the political system and the whole sphere of culture. Marx himself offered varying accounts of these interrelations, sometimes appearing to assert a strict economic determinism, generally attributing great importance to the progress of technology, especially in the capitalist era, and very often insisting on the causal primacy of the mode of production as a whole in 'determining' or 'conditioning' the entire social order (the classic statement of this position being in his Preface of 1859). Elsewhere, however, he expressed himself in terms which suggest a broader sociological view of the 'production of society', when he argued, for example, that the 'mode of production should not be regarded simply as the reproduction of the physical existence of individuals. It is far more a definite form of activity of these individuals, a definite way of expressing their life, a definite *mode of life*' (Marx and Engels 1845–6, vol. I, section IA).

Schumpeter was profoundly influenced by Marxist thought, but diverged from it in several important respects. First, he confined his analysis of economic development to the capitalist era, even setting aside – often in a dismissive way – questions concerning the origins of modern capitalism, and his general view of the place of historical studies in economics was never systematically expounded. True, in the discussion of method in his last work (1954) there is some emphasis on the value of economic history and economic sociology, but they are treated largely as separate, alternative approaches to economic questions. His substantive writings do not, for the most part, reveal any commitment to a theoretical model which would integrate historical sociology with economic analysis, but use historical data mainly in a descriptive fashion to illustrate economic development. It is true, of course, that Marx and most later Marxists also devoted their major studies to the development of modern industrial capitalism, but their analyses were always informed by a general theory of history that was distinctive in its broad outlines – and distinctively sociological in its emphasis on the class structure, the state and ideologies – even if still subject to diverse interpretation on many particular issues.

Secondly, Schumpeter had an entirely different conception of social classes – this being one of the most important sociological elements in his work – according to which the important feature was not the conflict between a rising and a declining class (which he thought Marxists grossly exaggerated), but the gradual decline of a dominant class through the loss of its social function. In the case of the developed capitalist societies of the twentieth century he argued, mistakenly as I have tried to show, that the decline of a particular social group – the entrepreneurs – would result in the displacement from its dominant position of the whole bourgeoisie or 'business class', and thus prepare the way for socialism.

But thirdly, Schumpeter also broached an important, more sociological criticism of Marxism, when he observed that the link between changes in the economic system and changes in the social order might be less direct and more tenuous than Marx, and Marxists generally, were inclined to believe, because social structures and attitudes, once having been formed, do not readily melt and may persist for centuries (see above, page 86). He did not, however, pursue this line of thought, and in his subsequent analysis tended to argue that the decline of capitalism and the advent of socialism, though not brought about solely by economic causes, would in fact create both a new economic system and a new social structure. The independent constraint exerted by long-established institutions and habits of mind seems to vanish from the picture, even though this is highly relevant to his later recognition that the march into socialism might perhaps come to a halt before attaining the goal envisaged by socialists.

It is here that we can see most clearly those elements in Marxist thought which influenced Schumpeter so strongly, notwithstanding his many reservations. The first is the conception of capitalism as an inherently dynamic economy which continually revolutionizes the system of production, mainly, if not exclusively, as a result of the successive revolutions in technology, which are in turn encouraged and stimulated by the needs of capitalist production. Modern industrial capitalism began with the steam engine, as Marx observed in a well-known aphorism, cited by Schumpeter (1942, p. 12) in a generally approving way; and Schumpeter's own theory of capitalist development is, to a large extent, a restatement in other terms – with the 'entrepreneur' replacing the 'capitalist' as the agent of innovation – of the Marxist view. There is also another close affinity insofar as both Marx and Schumpeter conceived the development of capitalism as a discontinuous and turbulent process. Marx, in one of his accounts of economic crises, wrote that 'From time to time the conflict of antagonistic agencies gives vent to crises. The crises are always only momentary and forcible solutions of the existing contradictions, violent eruptions which for a time restore the disturbed equilibrium' (*Capital*, vol. 3, ch. 15); and this strikingly resembles Schumpeter's notion of the 'gales of creative destruction' which periodically sweep over the capitalist economy. Furthermore, as we have seen (above, pages 65–7), Schumpeter, in his major study of business cycles, gave a pre-eminent place to the 'long waves' which had been conceptualized chiefly by Marxist economists.

There is a further link with Marxist thought in Schumpeter's exposition of the transition from capitalism to socialism, where he employed quite frequently the concept of an ineluctable 'socialization of the economy', noting explicitly that a large part of his argument about the development of capitalism 'may be summed up in the Marxian proposition that the economic process tends to socialize *itself*' (1942, p. 219). What he had in mind, however, was primarily the growth of large corporations, and this does not encompass the whole of Marx's conception, or the views of some later Marxists on the alternative possibilities that this process opened up. Marx outlined his own view in the manuscripts of the *Grundrisse* (1857–8) and of the third volume of *Capital* (1861–79). In the former he related socialization to the progress of science and technology, and in particular the advent of automated production, arguing that the creation of real wealth had come to depend, not on labour time, but on the application of science to production, and that as a result it is the human being's 'understanding of nature and his mastery over it by virtue of his existence as a social entity – in a word the development of the social individual – which now appears as the great foundation of production and wealth' (pp. 704–6). In *Capital* (vol. 3, chs 23 and 27) he concentrated on the changes in the role of capital in production, observing that 'money capital assumes a social character with the growth of credit', and that managers had begun to take over all the real functions of the investing capitalist, so that the whole process might be regarded as an 'abolition of the capitalist mode of production within capitalist production itself' – an idea not altogether remote from Schumpeter's view of the decline of capitalism. Elsewhere in *Capital* (vol. 3, ch. 15) Marx brought his conceptions of the socialization of capital and the socialization of labour together, when he described as two of the principal aspects of capitalist production (i) the concentration of means of production into a few hands, as a result of which they are no longer the property of the direct producers but are transformed into social powers of production, and (ii) the organization of labour itself as social labour, by co-operation, division of labour and the union of labour with the natural sciences.

Schumpeter, however, focused his attention mainly on the purely economic aspects of the concentration of capital in large corporations, influenced partly no doubt by the writings of Hilferding (1910) on the growth of trusts and cartels, though he neglected that part of the analysis which concerned the industrial role of the banks, and also by Hilferding's later articles (in the 1920s) on organized capitalism, in which the expanding economic role of the state, and the spread of 'partial planning' were emphasized. Hence, the movement towards socialism, as interpreted by Schumpeter, seemed to be the outcome of an economic process inherent in capitalism, the main effect of which was to eliminate competition and the entrepreneur, although the destructive criticism of the intellectuals also played some part. Marx's alternative conception, in which the concentration of capital is, to be sure, an important element – and is more adequately explained than in Schumpeter's largely descriptive account – also involved another element, the socialization of labour, as an essential precondition of socialism. In the *Grundrisse* Marx wrote about the future of human society in a more speculative fashion than was his habit elsewhere, and on one point at least he was realistic and accurate (and far ahead of other economists of his time) in foreseeing the development of automated production as a result of the progress of science, but his idea that one of the main consequences of this process would be to produce a general awareness, and more specifically a socialist consciousness, of the economy as a *social* enterprise which could be planned, co-ordinated and managed collectively by the producers themselves, raises many difficult questions. Marx himself referred on several occasions to co-operative associations, and in particular to the co-operative factories which represented 'within the old [capitalist] form the first sprouts of the new' (*Capital*, vol. 3, ch. 27; and see also Lowit 1962, Yeo 1991), but this provided no clue to the way of organizing a national economy, and in any case by the end of the nineteenth century economic development in the principal capitalist countries was actually taking quite a different course. During the first three decades of the twentieth century, therefore, Marxist thinkers became increasingly preoccupied with problems of the operation of a centrally planned economy (Bottomore 1990, chs 2 and 3), which also gave rise to the controversies about economic calculation in a socialist economy (see above, page 103) and entered into Schumpeter's discussion of socialism.

At the same time some Marxist thinkers became more aware that an economy dominated by large corporations and regulated by the state might evolve in several different directions, and this awareness is especially marked in Hilferding's writings. In the 1920s, when he was elaborating his conception of organized capitalism, Hilferding regarded it as a relatively stable system in which the economy was regulated and to some extent planned by the state and the large corporations, and as one which constituted a new starting-point for a gradual transition to socialism, involving a progressive subordination of the economy to the control of the democratic state. Subsequently, however, after the experience of Stalinism in the Soviet Union and of National Socialism in Germany, he became more acutely aware of the dangers arising from the growing power of the modern state itself, which was capable of producing, in one form or another, a totalitarian system (Hilferding 1940, 1941). Hence his insistence on the inseparability of socialism and democracy – socialism being in his view the core of the democratic movement – and his preliminary, unfinished sketch of a much-revised theory of the state which would necessarily have led him to consider how political power might be decentralized and a democratic ethos more widely diffused.

From Hilferding's writings, and to some extent from Schumpeter's brief account of the 'halfway house', we can derive a model of three principal forms in which a new socio-economic order might emerge from the continuing evolution of capitalism: (i) a socialist society conforming broadly with the aims of the socialist movement; (ii) a totalitarian system; and (iii) a corporatist, mixed-economy, welfare-capitalist society – though we should also not exclude the possibility, which has become more apparent during the past decade, of a partial return to an earlier type of *laissez-faire* capitalism. But before examining more closely these different possibilities, and the extent to which they have been realized, either wholly or partly, in actual social structures in the twentieth century, we should consider a third major achievement in the constitution of an economic sociology – that of Max Weber – which added another dimension to the discussion of these questions.

Like Schumpeter, but in an entirely different way, Weber was strongly affected by Marxist thought, more particularly because of its influence upon the rapidly growing socialist movement in Germany; and as a historian and sociologist he was primarily interested in the Marxist theory of history, in the social and cultural aspects of capitalism, and in the nature of socialism as an alternative form of society. In what is probably his best-known work (1904–5) Weber set out to show that an important factor in the development of modern capitalism was the diffusion of a capitalist 'spirit' owing much to the religious transformation which inculcated a new 'Protestant ethic'. His aim, however, was not 'to substitute for a one-sided materialistic an equally one-sided spiritualistic causal interpretation of culture and history', both of which were 'equally possible' (p. 183) as methodological approaches or initial hypotheses, but to establish more generally, as he argued in his writings on the methods of the social sciences, that history could be interpreted from different standpoints which are themselves conditioned by social and cultural values. Against the idea of a 'science of history', to which Marx clearly, and Schumpeter in a less explicit and more empiricist way, were committed, Weber asserted the possibility of diverse 'interpretations' based upon subjective value choices, embedded in more general cultural orientations, which in turn are affected by economic and political interests.[3]

Weber's account of the role of the Protestant ethic in the rise of capitalism has been much criticized by later scholars,[4] and it was rejected by Schumpeter on two different grounds. First, he argued that there was

> no such thing as a New Spirit of Capitalism in the sense that people would have had to acquire a new way of thinking in order to be able to transform a feudal economic world into a wholly different capitalist one. So soon as we realize that pure Feudalism and pure Capitalism are equally unrealistic creations of our own mind, the

problem of what it was that turned the one into the other vanishes completely. (1954, p. 80)

He then added in a footnote that

unfortunately, Max Weber lent the weight of his great authority to a way of thinking that has no other basis than a misuse of the method of Ideal Types. Accordingly, he set out to find an explanation for a process which sufficient attention to historical detail renders self-explanatory. (*ibid.*, n. 4)

Here Schumpeter's rather crude empiricist approach to historical questions shows itself most clearly, but it is somewhat mitigated by a second objection to the Weberian thesis which he formulated by saying that 'the whole of Max Weber's facts and arguments fits perfectly into Marx's system' (1942, p. 11).

In this form, however, the argument depended heavily upon Marx's theory of history, and neglected those aspects of social development – notably the fact that social structures, types and attitudes tend to persist and are not easily dissolved – which Schumpeter himself emphasized in the same text in expressing his reservations about the 'economic interpretation' (1942, p. 12). From this standpoint it may well be argued that the diffusion of a new rational, 'calculating' attitude did play a partly independent role in capitalist development, not as an antecedent condition but as a factor which was actively co-present with the economic changes. Elsewhere indeed Schumpeter made considerable use of Weber's more general conception of rationalization,[5] began his exposition of the theory of economic development by referring to 'the social process which rationalizes our life and thought' (1911, p. 57), and in his account of the decline of capitalism attributed great importance to the consequences of the rapid growth and diffusion of a rationalist and critical attitude (1942, Chapters 11 and 12; and see above, page 94).

Weber himself, in his *General Economic History* (published posthumously in 1923), gave a more comprehensive definition of capitalism (see above, page 100, Chapter 6, note 4), asserting, like Schumpeter, that the 'method of enterprise' was its fundamental characteristic, but also emphasizing its high degree of rationality (rational capital accounting, rational technology, calculable law) and incorporating into his definition the two principal criteria of the Marxist model, the private ownership of means of production and the sale of their labour power by propertyless workers (i.e. the transformation of labour power itself into a commodity). Moreover, in this final part of his book, devoted to the origin and development of modern capitalism, Weber not only analysed the economic processes involved, and the progress of technology, but also gave great prominence to the growth of cities and the national state, concluding that

> Out of this alliance of the state with capital, dictated by necessity, arose the national citizen class, the bourgeoisie in the modern sense of the word. Hence it is the closed national state which afforded to capitalism its chance for development – and as long as the national state does not give place to a world empire capitalism will also endure. (p. 249)

By contrast he gave very little attention here to the influence of the Protestant ethic, though still briefly asserting its importance: 'This development of the concept of the calling [or vocation] quickly gave to the modern entrepreneur a fabulously clear conscience, and industrious workers', and 'in comparison with it what the Renaissance did for capitalism shrinks into insignificance' (pp. 269–70).

In Weber's analysis of modern capitalism there are three features which distinguish his outlook very sharply from that of Marx or Schumpeter. First, his conception of the development of rationality was enlarged into, or derived from, a social 'vision' of the rationalization and 'disenchantment' of the world (Löwith 1932, Brubaker 1984) as a process which was already far advanced in the organization of work and in bureaucratic administration, and in his view would simply be given a further impetus in a socialist system. From this aspect Weber appears as a critic of capitalist civilization, but still more of the likely consequences of socialism, defending the integrity of the individual human being against the constraints of an 'iron cage' and the 'parcelling-out of the soul' in specialized functions.

But secondly, Weber's concern with the fate of the individual under capitalism or socialism was overshadowed to a large extent by his preoccupation with the nation state, and more especially with the situation and prospects of Germany as a 'world power'. In his inaugural lecture at Freiburg in 1895 he formulated the basic principle of his political theory as being the 'absolute primacy of the interests of the nation state' which constitute an 'ultimate standard of value' in both politics and economics (Weber 1971, pp. 14–15), and throughout his life he remained a passionate nationalist and imperialist who 'never envisaged any other world than his own, which was largely characterized by the rivalry of nation states' (Mommsen 1974, p. 37). From this value standpoint he considered that capitalism was the most effective economic basis for the growth of German power, while the bourgeoisie was the class most capable, in principle, of providing vigorous and responsible political leadership.[6]

A third distinctive feature in Weber's treatment of capitalism is that unlike Marx and Schumpeter he did not conceive it primarily as a dynamic, continually developing system, and there is in his analysis little or no reference to business cycles, the growth of large corporations, the role of banks or the effects of state intervention. Instead, after tracing the origins of capitalism and its establishment as the dominant economic system in Western Europe and North America during the second half of the nineteenth century, he then constructed an *a*historical model (most fully in his *General Economic History*) in a way which certainly laid him open to the charge which Schumpeter had brought of abusing the method of the 'ideal type' (see above, page 119). Weber himself (1921, ch. 2, prefatory note) disclaimed any intention of presenting an 'economic theory' of capitalism, saying that his work consisted 'only in an attempt to define certain concepts which are frequently used and to analyse some of the simplest sociological relationships in the economic sphere'. Nevertheless, his 'ideal type' of capitalism was itself defective as a starting-point for such an enquiry insofar as it did not take any account of the profound structural changes in the capitalist economy that were already very evident at the beginning of the twentieth century, or of the turbulent character of this unceasing process of change.

Because Weber largely ignored the recent changes in the capitalist economy he was also less concerned than was Schumpeter with any process of 'socialization' which might lead towards socialism, and in particular he dismissed the idea that the war economy would have such an outcome. His writings on, and in opposition to, socialism were focused on three main issues. First, he argued (1921, p. 194) that 'competition on the market is an essential condition of the existence of rational money accounting', and in a brief critical reference to Otto Neurath's (1919) conception of 'accounting in kind' he emphasized the importance, from a technical point of view, of 'accurate calculation' and suggested that 'a limit to the possible degree of socialization would be set by the necessity of maintaining a system of effective prices' (1921, p. 207). Thus he was one of the first scholars to raise, as an objection to socialism, the problem of 'socialist calculation' which became a focal point of controversy in the 1920s and 1930s in the writings of Mises and Hayek.[7] Schumpeter, as we have seen (above, page 57) rejected this kind of argument, largely on the basis of the studies by Barone and Oskar Lange.

The second issue concerned bureaucracy, which Weber thought a socialist system would greatly extend: 'the administration of nationalized or "socialized" enterprises too would become bureaucratic . . . If private capitalism were eliminated the state bureaucracy would rule *alone*' (1918a, pp. 331–2), and the eventual outcome would be a 'dictatorship of the official' (1918b, p. 508). On this point too Schumpeter disagreed, noting how far, in a capitalist economy partly socialized by the growth of large corporations, 'the bureaucratization of economic life – of life in general even – has gone already', and then arguing that 'bureaucracy is not an obstacle to democracy but an inevitable complement to it' (1942, p. 206). What neither Weber nor Schumpeter envisaged, however, was the specific form that bureaucracy would assume in the one-party regimes of communist societies where the so-called 'dictatorship of the proletariat' became in reality the dictatorship of *party* officials.

The third issue was presented by Weber from the standpoint of his own scheme of value preferences, in which the nation state had a pre-eminent place. He concluded his lecture on socialism (1918b), which was based largely on Bernstein's (1899) exposition of the aims of democratic socialism in the changing socio-economic conditions of the late nineteenth century, by saying that 'The question is whether this socialism will be of such a kind that it is bearable from the standpoint of the interests of the state, and in particular at the present time, of its military interests'. This was the tenor of much of his political writing during the last two years of his life, in which he expressed his concern that the socialist movement, and especially its revolutionary wing, would weaken still further the German state, and insisted that the overriding consideration must be the creation of a strong and effective political leadership.

It was in this context that Weber formulated his particular conception of democracy, with which the alternative theory of democracy outlined by Schumpeter has significant affinities, and by which it may well have been inspired. At all events, both thinkers rejected major elements in the 'classical doctrine', such as the idea of government *by* the people or of a process of gradually extending democracy towards more direct participation in government,[8] and conceived democracy as a method or institutional arrangement for selecting representatives, leaders or governments. There were, however, some differences. Schumpeter (1942, p. 273) argued that 'the primary function of the electors' vote is to produce government', and he did not emphasize unduly the role of 'leadership' (p. 273, n. 9), whereas Weber was increasingly preoccupied with 'charismatic' leaders who would counter the tendency towards bureaucratization and effectively promote the power interests of the nation state. In his view the modern mass democracies could only take the form of 'plebiscitarian leader democracies' (1919; and see Mommsen 1974, ch. 4).

From the work of Marx, Weber and Schumpeter there emerged styles of economic sociology in which Marxist thought had a pre-eminent place. Insofar as Marx formulated a sociological theory of history in which the mode of production was conceived as the basic factor determining or conditioning a whole 'form of life', his ideas provided the starting-point and the framework for all later studies in this field.[9] Schumpeter followed this Marxist model closely when he argued that 'the economic world is relatively autonomous because it takes up such a great part of a nation's life, and forms or conditions a great part of the remainder' (1911, p. 58), and accepted as 'invaluable working hypotheses' the propositions that modes of production 'have a logic of their own' and are the 'fundamental determinants of social structures', the latter in turn breeding 'attitudes, actions and civilizations' (1942, p. 13). Indeed, reading Schumpeter's work as a whole, one has an impression not only of the enormous fascination that Marxist thought exercised on him, and his indebtedness to it, but also that in an important sense he was engaged throughout his life in a great intellectual struggle to avoid succumbing to it completely – for example, by rejecting in principle the idea of class conflict as a major factor in social development, though in particular situations he recognized its importance; or by noting in one context the durability of social structures through periods of economic change, while arguing elsewhere that the 'socialization' of the economy was in fact creating a new type of society. All of which makes any account of Schumpeter's basic conceptions which ignores their relation to Marxist theory entirely superficial.

Weber was more directly critical of Marxism and of socialism. He rejected the Marxist claim to have established a comprehensive causal explanation of historical development, but at the same time recognized that the 'materialist conception of history' had been, and if freed from dogma would long remain, an illuminating and fertile scientific principle. Hence his insistence on the economic *interpretation* of history as one of the most important aims of sociological or socio-economic enquiry, and the devotion of a great part of his own work to an investigation of the relationship between economic structures and other forms of social association, ranging from social classes and political systems to diverse cultural forms, especially religious ideas and practices. In *Economy and Society* he undertook a comprehensive analysis of the sociological categories of economic action (far more thorough than anything to be found in Schumpeter's economic sociology) and went on to examine types of domination and authority, classes, status groups and parties, the historical forms of human society in relation to the economy, the sociological aspects of law, the role of towns in different economies and civilizations, and the development of bureaucratic administration. Much of this analysis reveals his preoccupation with Marxist themes, particularly his discussion of a market economy and socialism, of classes as major potential sources of communal action in modern capitalist society, and of the social bases of political power. Furthermore, in his *General Economic History* he incorporated into his definition of capitalism (see above, page 100, Chapter 6, note 4) fundamental Marxist conceptions, and it may also be argued that the emphasis which he laid upon nation states and the struggle between them was a recognition, from a different value perspective, of the same phenomenon which Marxists were analysing in their theories of imperialism. But on the question of socialism Weber took a very different view from that of Marx or Schumpeter. First, he did not expect it to replace capitalism, and certainly did not desire this outcome, or even see any relative merit in it; secondly, he considered that a socialist economy and society would not be viable, in anything like the form anticipated by socialists, because rational calculation (and hence economic progress) would be impossible in a planned economy, and because the state bureaucracy would come to dominate society (see above, page 122).

Weber's relation to Marxist thought was complex, and it has still not been fully explored.[10] But Marxism was undoubtedly a salient feature of the intellectual and political milieu in which Weber's own conceptions were formed, and it is not unreasonable to claim, as I did in a previous study, that 'the greater part of Weber's sociology can be read . . . as a prolonged and varied commentary upon the Marxist theory' (Bottomore 1978, p. 129).[11] Manifestly, for much of his life, Weber (like Schumpeter) was preoccupied with those questions about the nature of a capitalist economy, the kind of society and civilization that it tended to create, its internal problems (and even contradictions), and the possibility that it would eventually be transformed into a socialist order, which Marx had been the first to pose in a compelling fashion. Broadly then, we can say that the studies of, and controversies about, capitalism and socialism have formed the central core of economic sociology, and even of whole sociological systems, since the middle of the nineteenth century; but before going on to consider how far that is still the case today it is necessary to take account of an alternative theoretical scheme which also has one of its main sources in Weber's thought.

The idea of the 'rationalization' of the modern world, as a process which was, to be sure, closely connected with the development of capitalism but according to Weber would be just as inescapable, and even more extensive, in a socialist society, was one from which there could be derived conceptions of 'industrialization' and 'modernization' as the crucial features of social development in the twentieth century. Industrialization, of course, was by no means an entirely novel conception – the advent of 'industrial society' had been proclaimed long before by Saint-Simon, Comte and Spencer, and in another fashion by Marx – but over the past half-century it has acquired a new significance in several different ways. First, industrial society, defined as a society 'in which large-scale industry . . . is the characteristic form of production' (Aron 1967a, p. 73), and where science and technology have an increasingly dominant role, came to be regarded by many social scientists as the fundamental socio-economic phenomenon of the age, in relation to which capitalism and socialism might be represented simply as alternative ways of carrying on the process of rapid economic growth, to be judged, at any rate in part, by their success in that endeavour. Industrial society is also 'a type of society which appears to open up a new era in human experience' (Aron 1967b, p. 97), and from that standpoint the decisive moment in human history can be more convincingly represented as a transition from pre-industrial to industrial society than by that historical schema which conceptualizes social development in terms of a movement from feudalism to capitalism and then to socialism.

Secondly, however, in the post-colonial situation after the Second World War, the division between the industrially advanced countries and those of the pre-industrial 'third world' came to be conceived by many social scientists as one between 'modern' and 'traditional' societies, and the process of development in the 'underdeveloped' countries as a comprehensive modernization of their economies, political systems and cultures. The theories of modernization, strongly influenced by Weber's typology of social action (1921, ch. 1, sect. 2; and see also Brubaker 1984, ch. 2), particularly as this was interpreted, expanded and systematized by Parsons (1951), were, however, increasingly criticized from the 1960s insofar as they purported to provide an explanatory model of economic and social development (see Larrain 1989, pp. 98–102). A German historian of an earlier phase of modernization within Western capitalism noted that the term is vague, and that 'there is growing scepticism about its explanatory value', but suggested that 'it may be useful to work with a more empirical, descriptive concept of "modernity" and "modernization" ' (Peukert 1991, p. 81). Used in this way modernity refers descriptively to 'fully fledged industrial society', characterized economically by 'highly rationalized . . . production, complex technological infrastructures and a substantial degree of bureaucratized administrative and service activity'; socially by 'the division of labour, wage and salary discipline, an urbanized environment, extensive educational opportunities and a demand for skills and training'; culturally by the domination of media products, and the breaking of continuity with 'traditional aesthetic principles and practices'; and intellectually by 'the triumph of western rationality, whether in social planning, the expansion of the sciences or the self-replicating dynamism of technology, although this optimism is accompanied by sceptical doubts from social thinkers and cultural critics' (*ibid.*, p. 82).

Modernity, conceived in this way, evidently refers not to a static, but to a dynamic, continuously developing form of society, and the currently fashionable notion of 'post-modernity' becomes more intelligible, though still vague and frequently obscure, if it is seen as a description of a further stage in this process, at least in some of its aspects. The development of industrial society, like that of capitalism – with which it has been historically most closely associated – in the theories of Marx and Schumpeter, is also a turbulent, tension-ridden process,[12] whether it takes place in advanced capitalist societies, in socialist societies of the former Soviet type, or in newly industrializing countries. No one can doubt that it is the successive transformations of the system of production which have largely shaped the world we inhabit at the end of the twentieth century, or that their potent influence will continue in the foreseeable future. In this sense, not only are industrialization, modernization and rationalization necessarily central concerns of economic sociology, but an 'economic interpretation' of present-day societies provides one of the most secure foundations for general sociology.

Any such interpretation, however, if it is to go beyond a purely descriptive account, has to deal with difficult questions concerning the causal or quasi-causal (i.e. mediated by human consciousness and action) connections between different elements in the process of development, the tensions and conflicts which it generates, the various phases and the cyclical character of capitalist economic development, and the possibility that capitalism, because of some inherent instability as a social order, will eventually be superseded by a different economic system (as another form of industrial society) which could be called socialist. There were important differences between Marx and later Marxists, Weber and Schumpeter in the way that these central issues were conceived and analysed, though all of them were mainly preoccupied with industrialization and its consequences, and with *the* great social question of capitalism and socialism as alternative types of industrial society.

In the case of Weber, as I have indicated, the model of capitalism was largely static (ignoring business cycles and the growth of large corporations) and the main dynamic elements in his theoretical scheme were the continuing rationalization of social life (owing as much, or more, to the spread of bureaucratic administration as to the technical organization of production) and the rivalry between nation states. Schumpeter was much closer to Marxist theory in his conception of capitalist development as a process of continual though irregular innovation and change, marked by 'gales of creative destruction', and in his emphasis on the progressive socialization of the economy, but he diverged from that theory in his account of the forces which might bring about a transition to socialism; whereas Weber, on this point, seems more 'Marxist' insofar as he regarded the opposition between capitalism and socialism as a political struggle between the parties of the bourgeoisie and the working class. But Schumpeter also differed both from Weber and from the Marxists when he suggested briefly, in his last writings, that the movement towards socialism might lose momentum and come to rest at some 'halfway house', though he did not rate this possibility very highly or, consequently, go on to consider whether such an intermediate type of economy and society might prove to be relatively stable.

Fifty years have passed since the last of these major theoretical analyses were expounded, and we now need to re-examine, in the light of the profound economic and social changes that have taken place, the issues that were posed and came to dominate the controversies in economic sociology from the end of the nineteenth century. And first we have to consider whether the opposition between capitalism and socialism remains a central question for theoretical analysis and empirical research. This was undoubtedly still the case in the decade immediately following the Second World War, when the movement towards socialism became more pronounced in Western Europe (and Schumpeter, in his post-war writings, noted its early manifestations), as well as in some Third World countries. But several factors then began to change this situation. One was the reconstruction of European capitalism as 'welfare capitalism', due partly to the growing influence of the labour movement, but partly also to more general changes in social attitudes during and after the war, which led to a new emphasis being placed on the elimination of poverty and on the development of a broader conception of citizenship in which social rights were given prominence (see Marshall 1950).

A second important factor was the economic success of this post-war capitalism. Schumpeter had always insisted that capitalism would not decline as a result of economic failure, but because of its success in rationalizing and socializing the economy, and promoting economic growth; in the course of which, however, it also engendered a critical attitude towards, and gradually undermined, its own social order. In the period from 1950 to 1973 this economic success was greater than ever before, but it took place in a system that was more 'organized' (in Hilferding's sense, which Schumpeter largely adopted), partially planned and more 'socialistic' in several respects; so that capitalism was far more successful in a broader economic sense (avoiding recession and maintaining full employment), thus escaping, to a large extent, some of the specific criticisms that could be made of the capitalism of the 1930s. In this new capitalist order the changes in the economic structure and their connection with exceptionally high rates of growth were crucial elements, and there was no such general erosion of bourgeois values as Schumpeter had anticipated (see above, page 94). On the contrary, it may be argued that the changes had a greater impact on socialist values and the socialist movement, as a consequence of the expansion of the middle class and some degree of *'embourgeoisement'* of the working class.

But there is also a third major factor in post-war development to be taken into account: namely, the phenomenon of self-styled 'real socialism' in Eastern Europe. In the Soviet Union and in the other countries where a Soviet-type system had been imposed at the end of the war, harsh political dictatorships managed centrally planned economies and controlled all aspects of social life; and insofar as they could be represented as socialist not only by their own political leaders and ideologists but also by the Western media, they had a strongly deterrent effect on any policies that envisaged a further advance towards socialism – however different and democratic it could claim to be – in the capitalist countries. From the 1970s, moreover, the Soviet-type systems faced increasing internal difficulties and opposition, and their collapse since 1989 has been hailed by many Western commentators as the 'death of socialism', although it would be more accurate to speak of the demise of totalitarian regimes which had exploited and deformed socialist ideas in order to construct a state ideology that served as an instrument of domination.

The first issue to be considered here is whether these economic and social transformations of the post-war era should be interpreted as a new stage in the development of capitalism, in which both the economy and the social order have a greater stability than Schumpeter envisaged, or as the emergence of a new kind of socio-economic system which is located somewhere between capitalism and socialism. If Schumpeter had been setting out to write his study of capitalism and socialism some thirty or forty years later he would doubtless have paid greater attention to the possibility of his halfway house becoming rather more like a permanent residence than a mere transit camp; and many social scientists, from the 1950s to the 1970s, did adopt such a view in their conceptualizations of welfare capitalism, the mixed economy, corporatism or the social market economy. But there are several reasons for questioning whether this kind of economy and social order had in fact the long-term stability that was often attributed to it. To begin with, these mixed economies (primarily in Europe) were still predominantly capitalist, although there was more extensive public ownership and a greater degree of public control and planning in some countries than in others; hence they were still not immune to the fluctuations of the business cycle, as has become abundantly clear in the recession, now perhaps turning into a severe depression, that began in the 1980s. Further, there were always powerful capitalist groups which wanted to roll back the frontiers of public ownership and the welfare state, and their efforts, besides having their most conspicuous success so far in the privatizations carried out in Britain over the past decade, have also exerted a wider influence in propagating the virtues of 'free market', more *laissez-faire* economies and decrying what is called a 'dependency culture'. In addition, the welfare state has had to face increasing fiscal problems as a consequence of declining growth rates, rising unemployment and ageing populations.

Schumpeter himself, in a study (1918) occasioned by discussions of a possible 'crisis of the tax-state' following the growth of public debt during the First World War, outlined a sociology of public finance, or fiscal sociology, which raised important questions about the relation between the tax-state and the private enterprise economy (see above, page 54). With the massive growth of public expenditure since the Second World War these issues have assumed still greater importance, particularly in conditions of economic recession, but this area of economic sociology has been badly neglected, and the literature on the subject is relatively sparse. One valuable recent study is that by Musgrave (1988), who outlines very clearly several alternative approaches to the question (especially by Marxist writers) and summarizes the causes which have been suggested as tending to produce a fiscal crisis, while rejecting the view that such a crisis is bound to occur. There is evidently a need for much more extensive research and analysis in this field, which could be most fruitfully pursued in a theoretical framework that recognized the existence of two opposed tendencies in modern industrial societies: one towards inequality as an outcome of the operation of a capitalist economy, the other towards greater equality as a consequence of the development of citizenship and the enlargement of social rights in the welfare state.[13]

The problems of the welfare state, the continuing instability of capitalism manifested in the cycle of expansion and depression (with all its social consequences), the resurgence in some countries of doctrines and policies of unfettered free-market capitalism, and increasing popular discontent with the results that flow from the implementation of such policies, all show that the confrontation between capitalism and socialism continues to be a major element in social and political conflicts. This is not only apparent in the developed capitalist countries, but also in Eastern Europe, where many of the post-communist regimes have adopted, for various reasons, extreme policies of privatization and the abandonment of planning which have so far resulted in economic devastation, provoking widespread disillusionment and the gradual re-emergence of a socialist opposition. Economic sociology has still, therefore, to be largely concerned with the kind of issues that preoccupied Schumpeter (and with the Marxist analyses which formed the background of his work), and in particular with the question whether, after all, the halfway house is not a final destination but simply a further stage in a slow transition to an entirely different type of economy and society.

In pursuing such enquiries, however, many problems arise concerning the nature and feasibility of socialism itself. It can be taken for granted that the kind of highly centralized totalitarian system which called itself 'socialist' is now an extinct species, but there are numerous issues concerning other forms of socialism – more controversial, in some respects, after the collapse of the East European regimes – among the most prominent being those that relate to public ownership and planning. On those subjects I have written elsewhere (Bottomore 1990), and here I will only remark that they constitute vast fields of study to which far more systematic empirical research could usefully be devoted, dealing with such questions as the relative efficiency and capacity for innovation of public and private enterprises, and the achievements and limitations of economic and social planning. At present, both these subjects are enveloped in a fog of unexamined popular folklore, some of which finds its way into the textbooks, and informed discussion of them is inhibited by the lack of fundamental research. As Hammond (1984, pp. 37–8) has commented with reference to efficiency:

> casual impressions are not to be trusted. The only way I can think of to see whether public or private enterprise really is more efficient would be to make a very careful international comparison of, say, the electricity industry in private hands in the U.S., and in public hands almost anywhere else. And do the same for a number of other such industries too . . .. In any case, whether or not the myth that public enterprises are less efficient has any reality, we still want to ask as economists if there is any good reason for public enterprises to be less efficient.'

One very suitable case for major research at the present time would be the effects of privatization on the British economy, which, to judge by 'casual impressions', do not seem to have been a brilliant success.

But this opposition between capitalism and socialism, however large the space that it should still occupy, is far from exhausting the subject matter of economic sociology today. In the first place, it is embedded in, and profoundly affected by, the massive economic changes generated by the continuing rapid advance of science and technology: the transformation of the occupational structure and the nature of work, the development of giant multinational corporations, the rationalization and internationalization of mass production and mass consumption. Economic development now takes place on a world scale, and everywhere it is regulated in one way or another by governments, increasingly

The realm of economic sociology 133

through regional and international, intergovernmental agreements and agencies. In this process, to be sure, the advanced capitalist countries, and particular 'lead' countries at different times – the USA for much of the post-war period, Japan and Germany (the latter within the European Community) more recently and for the foreseeable future – have had a predominant influence; but this is a new kind of capitalism in which state intervention and regulation have a substantial role, and post-war economic development has been characterized especially by the trend towards increased public control and planning, and various reactions against this trend, expressed in the alternative policies of mainly class-based parties.[14]

There are, however, two other issues, arising directly from the high rates of growth in the industrial countries since the war, which now constitute major areas of economic sociology. The first is the great gulf, which has tended to widen rather than contract, between rich and poor countries, and the complex of problems that this poses concerning not only the historical causes of the disparity, but also the conditions in which, and the policies through which, it might be overcome. As I noted earlier (see above, page 126) the issue has frequently been conceptualized in terms of 'modernization', but many recent studies have diverged from this approach, emphasizing the importance of indigenous paths of development, and also the different consequences for 'developing countries' of more 'capitalistic' or more 'socialistic' development policies.[15]

The second issue concerns the effects of rapid economic growth on the environment, including the destruction of plant and animal species, pollution of all kinds and global warming. The scale of such problems in the future can be most clearly visualized if we suppose, as I have suggested elsewhere (Bottomore 1990, p. 133):

> that every country eventually attained living standards equal to those in the prosperous West European societies [in which case] economic development on this scale, coupled with population growth, would place an enormous burden on the earth's resources . . . and would add massively to the problems of pollution.

Such considerations have already generated more critical attitudes to economic growth and more extensive discussion of an alternative, sustainable type of economy.[16]

These new issues, while they extend greatly the field of study of economic sociology, can nevertheless be brought within the framework of a very general paradigm which has its principal sources in some versions of Marxist social theory and in Schumpeter's writings. The idea of 'socialization', introduced by Marx, elaborated by Hilferding in his conception of the 'organized' economy and adopted by Schumpeter, has implications going beyond the economic sphere, some of which Marx outlined in the *Grundrisse* (see above, page 115). The underlying conception which it expresses is that 'socialized humanity' (to use Max Adler's term), with the development of the economy and what Schumpeter referred to in his discussion of the tax-state as the 'consequent expansion of the sphere of social sympathy', becomes increasingly capable, and desirous, of managing its economic and social affairs collectively, for the benefit of all members of society. This provides an invaluable 'guiding thread' for explaining the manifest growth of collective regulation and the collective provision of goods and services in the industrial countries since 1945, and for analysing the new problems of inequality between nations and of the protection of the environment, which clearly require for their solution a further extension of 'social sympathy' and a more precise conception – ultimately to be embodied in appropriate social institutions – of a socialized, collectively responsible humanity on a world scale.

But if economic sociology is to follow this course it has also to become more sociological, in a more systematic and critical way. Class relations and the political conflicts arising from them, which occupy a central place in Marxist theory as a major factor in the process of collectivization, assume new forms as a result of changes in the occupational and class structure, and of the wider consequences of economic growth. Furthermore, the persistence of elements inherited from earlier social structures and attitudes, which Schumpeter sometimes emphasized but on other occasions seemed to forget, may have a retarding effect on the development of a more collectivist outlook, while economic growth itself also promotes a contrary development of certain kinds of individualism, so that there is a fluctuating balance between the two tendencies and continuing controversy about their interrelationship. The institutions and mechanisms of collective regulation themselves give rise to further problems concerning, for example,

The realm of economic sociology 135

the spread of bureaucratic administration and the emergence of new hierarchies, whether in large productive enterprises or at the level of national and international planning. In these areas, and in many others, a great deal of new research has to be undertaken, which can be pursued most effectively, I have argued, by adopting as our starting-point the development of the system of production, conceived as the centre of an intricate web of social relations. In short, we should begin, as did Schumpeter, from a critically revised economic interpretation of history, though we may in due course be led to some different conclusions.

Notes

1. See particularly Hilferding (1941, p. 111), who observed that this 'unfortunate designation has been responsible, in no small degree, for repeated misunderstandings and sterile polemics', and argued that while Marx, in his initial critical encounter with Hegelian philosophy, had opposed his 'materialist' conception to idealist speculation, 'in reality [as Marx himself later insisted] it is a matter of the opposition between scientific enquiry and philosophical speculation. The object of this enquiry makes Marx's conception of history a *sociological* conception of history.'
2. See Engels (1892, Introduction).
3. Weber expressed this view in various ways in his essay on 'objectivity', published in the *Archiv für Sozialwissenschaft und Sozialpolitik* at the time when he became one of its editors, observing that 'the analysis of social and cultural phenomena with special reference to their economic conditioning and effects was a scientific principle of creative fruitfulness', and that while 'the so-called "materialist conception of history" as a *Weltanschauung* or as a formula for the causal explanation of historical reality is to be rejected most emphatically ... the advancement of the economic *interpretation* of history is one of the most important aims of our journal' (1904, p. 68). And in concluding his essay he wrote that 'there comes a moment when the perspective changes .... The light of the great cultural problems moves on. Then science too prepares to change its standpoint and its conceptual apparatus and to look down upon the stream of events from the heights of thought' (p. 112).
4. For a general discussion see G. Marshall (1982).
5. On the complexities of this conception see Brubaker (1984).
6. Weber was, however, particularly concerned by the fact that Bis-

marck's rule and the power of the state bureaucracy in Imperial Germany had reduced the bourgeoisie to a condition of political immaturity and impotence (see especially Weber 1918a; and also Bottomore 1984, ch. 7).
7. In a footnote (1921, p. 211, n. 42) Weber referred to the early article by Mises (1920) on this subject, which had appeared in the *Archiv für Sozialwissenschaft und Sozialpolitik*, vol. 47, while his (Weber's) own book was in press.
8. Schumpeter's view is discussed above (page 108). Weber, in a letter of 1908 to Roberto Michels (cited in Mommsen 1959), declared that 'any idea which proposes to eliminate the domination of man by man through an extension of "democracy" is utopian'.
9. Besides Weber and Schumpeter, whose writings, however, have had by far the greatest impact on all subsequent research and debate, there were many other social scientists whose contributions to the subject, influenced to a greater or lesser extent by Marxist thought, would need to be taken into account in a wider study. Among the more important were the economists of the German historical school and in particular Sombart; Durkheim and especially his more 'socialistic' followers, Simiand, Mauss and Halbwachs; and scholars such as Polanyi and Veblen. There is a short general survey of these and other contributions in Swedberg (1987, pp. 11–62).
10. The most illuminating attempt so far is to be found in the short early study by Löwith (1932). But there is also a useful discussion in Schroeter's introduction to Antonio and Glassman (eds), *A Weber–Marx Dialogue* (1985), though the book itself does not quite live up to its title since almost all the contributors engage in the dialogue from positions that are generally favourable to Weber's ideas, while basic conceptions in Marxist thought remain unexpressed.
11. See also the comment by Fleischmann (1964, p. 194) that 'it was probably Marx who exerted the most profound and lasting influence on Weber'.
12. See Peukert 1991, ch. 3 for an illuminating account of one particular case.
13. For a more comprehensive discussion, see Marshall and Bottomore (1992).
14. On the changes that have occurred in class relations and class politics, see Bottomore (1991a, ch. 5); and on the capitalist class in particular, Bottomore and Brym (1989).
15. For a general discussion of different approaches, see Larrain (1989).
16. For a wide-ranging study of ecological economics, see Martinez-Alier (1987).

BIBLIOGRAPHY

Aaron, H.J. and Boskin, M. (eds) 1980, *The Economics of Taxation* (Washington, DC: The Brookings Institution).
Adler, M. 1904, *Kausalität und Teleologie im Streite um die Wissenschaft* (Vienna: Wiener Volksbuchhandlung Ignaz Brand).
Adler, M. 1919, *Georg Simmels Bedeutung für die Geistesgeschichte* (Vienna and Leipzig: Anzengruber-Verlag).
Adler, M. 1925, *Kant und der Marxismus* (Berlin: E. Laub'sche Verlagsbuchhandlung).
Adler, M. 1933, 'Metamorphosis of the working class?', *Der Kampf*, 26, pp. 367–82, 406–14 (English trans. in Bottomore, T. and Goode, P. (eds) 1978).
Agassi, J. 1966, 'Methodological individualism', *British Journal of Sociology*, 11,3.
Amsden, A.H. 1987, 'Imperialism', in Eatwell, J. *et al.* (eds) 1987.
Antonio, R.J. and Glassman, R.M. (eds) 1985, *A Weber-Marx Dialogue* (Lawrence, KS: University Press of Kansas).
Aron, R. 1958, *War and Industrial Society* (London: Oxford University Press).
Aron, R. 1967a, *18 Lectures on Industrial Society* (London: Weidenfeld & Nicolson).
Aron, R. 1967b, *The Industrial Society* (London: Weidenfeld & Nicolson).

Barea, I. 1966, *Vienna* (London: Secker & Warburg).
Barone, E. 1908, 'The ministry of production in a collectivist state', in Hayek, F.A. (ed.) 1935.
Bauer, O. 1907, *Die Nationalitätenfrage und die Sozialdemokratie* (2nd edn. Vienna: Wiener Volksbuchhandlung, 1924).

Bauer, O. 1919, *Der Weg zum Sozialismus* (Vienna: Wiener Volksbuchhandlung).
Bauer, O. 1931, *Kapitalismus und Sozialismus nach dem Weltkrieg*, vol. 1, *Rationalisierung oder Fehlrationalisierung?* (Vienna: Wiener Volksbuchhandlung).
Beetham, D. 1983, *Marxists in Face of Fascism* (Manchester: Manchester University Press).
Berner, P., Brix, E. and Mantl, W. (eds) 1986, *Wien um 1900; Aufbruch in der Moderne* (Vienna: Verlag für Geschichte und Politik).
Bernstein, E. 1899, *Evolutionary Socialism* (New York: Schocken, 1961).
Bhaskar, R. 1991, 'Determinism', in Bottomore, T. (ed.) 1991b.
Böhm-Bawerk, E. von 1924, *Gesammelte Schriften*, ed. F.X. Weisz (Vienna and Leipzig: Holder-Pichler-Tempsky).
Bottomore, T. 1975, *Sociology as Social Criticism* (London: Allen & Unwin).
Bottomore, T. 1978, 'Marxism and sociology', in Bottomore, T. and Nisbet, R. (eds) 1978.
Bottomore, T. 1981, 'The decline of capitalism, sociologically considered', in Heertje, A. (ed.) 1981.
Bottomore, T. 1984, *Sociology and Socialism* (Brighton: Wheatsheaf).
Bottomore, T. 1984, *Theories of Modern Capitalism* (London: Allen & Unwin).
Bottomore, T. 1990, *The Socialist Economy: Theory and practice* (Hemel Hempstead: Harvester Wheatsheaf).
Bottomore, T. 1991a, *Classes in Modern Society* (2nd edn London: HarperCollins).
Bottomore, T. (ed.) 1991b, *A Dictionary of Marxist Thought* (2nd edn Oxford: Blackwell).
Bottomore, T. and Brym, R. (eds) 1989, *The Capitalist Class: An international study* (Hemel Hempstead: Harvester Wheatsheaf).
Bottomore, T. and Nisbet, R. (eds) 1978, *A History of Sociological Analysis* (New York: Basic Books).
Bottomore, T. and Goode, P. (eds) 1978, *Austro-Marxism* (Oxford: Clarendon Press).
Braunthal, J. 1967, *History of the International, 1914–1943* (London: Nelson).
Brewer, A. 1980, *Marxist Theories of Imperialism* (London: Routledge & Kegan Paul).
Brubaker, R. 1984, *The Limits of Rationality: An essay on the social and moral thought of Max Weber* (London: Allen & Unwin).
Brym, R.J. 1980, *Intellectuals and Politics* (London: Allen & Unwin).
Bukharin, N. 1915, *Imperialism and World Economy* (London: Merlin Press, 1972).

Caldwell, B.J. (ed.) 1990, *Carl Menger and his Legacy in Economics* (Durham and London: Duke University Press).
Csáky, M. 1986, 'Die sozial-kulturelle Wechselwirkung in der Zeit des Wiener Fin de siècle. Versuch einer Deutung', in Berner, P. *et al.* (eds) 1986.
Eatwell, J., Milgate, M. and Newman, P. (eds) 1987, *The New Palgrave: A dictionary of economics* (London: Macmillan).
Engels, F. 1892, 'Introduction' to the English edn of *Socialism: Utopian and Scientific*. Reprinted in various collected writings.
Fellner, W. 1981, 'March into socialism, or viable postwar stage of capitalism?', in Heertje, A. (ed.) 1981.
Fleischmann, E. 1964, 'De Weber à Nietzsche', *European Journal of Sociology*, V, 2, pp. 190–238.
Freeman, C. 1990, 'Schumpeter's *Business Cycles* revisited', in Heertje, A. and Perlman, M. (eds) 1990.
Fusfeld, D.R. 1987, 'Methodenstreit', in Eatwell, J. *et al.* (eds) 1987.
Godelier, M. 1977, *Perspectives in Marxist Anthropology* (Cambridge: Cambridge University Press).
Goldscheid, R. 1917, *Staatssozialismus oder Staatskapitalismus*. Reprinted in Goldscheid, R. and Schumpeter, J. *Die Finanzkrise des Steuerstaats: Beiträge zur politischen Ökonomie der Staatsfinanzen*, ed. R. Hickel (Frankfurt: Suhrkamp, 1976).
Goodwin, R.M. 1990, 'Walras and Schumpeter: the vision reaffirmed', in Heertje, A. and Perlman, M. (eds) 1990.
Gordon, D.M. 1980, 'Stages of accumulation and long economic cycles', in Hopkins, T.K. and Wallerstein, I. (eds), *Processes of the World-System* (Beverly Hills, CA and London: Sage Publications).
Gulick, C.A. 1948, *Austria from Habsburg to Hitler* (Berkeley and Los Angeles, CA: University of California Press).
Habermas, J. 1979, *Communication and the Evolution of Society* (London: Heinemann).
Hammond, P.J. 1984, 'Is entrepreneurship obsolescent?', in Seidl, C. (ed.) 1984.
Hanusch, H. (ed.) 1988, *Evolutionary Economics* (Cambridge: Cambridge University Press).
Harris, L. 1991, 'Finance capital', in Bottomore, T. (ed.) 1991b.
Harris, S.E. (ed.) 1951, *Schumpeter, Social Scientist* (Cambridge, MA: Harvard University Press).
Hayek, F.A. (ed.) 1935, *Collectivist Economic Planning* (London: Routledge).
Heath, A. 1981, *Social Mobility* (London; Fontana).

Heertje, A. (ed.) 1981, *Schumpeter's Vision* (Eastbourne and New York: Praeger).
Heertje, A. and Perlman, M. (eds) 1990, *Evolving Technology and Market Structure* (Ann Arbor, MI: University of Michigan Press).
Hegedüs, A. 1976, *Socialism and Bureaucracy* (London: Allison & Busby).
Heller, E. 1952, *The Disinherited Mind* (London: Bowes & Bowes).
Hilferding, R. 1904, *Böhm-Bawerks Marx-Kritik* (English trans. in Sweezy, P. (ed.), New York: Augustus M. Kelley, 1949).
Hilferding, R. 1910, *Finance Capital: A study of the latest phase of capitalist development* (London: Routledge & Kegan Paul, 1981).
Hilferding, R. 1927, 'Die Aufgaben der Sozialdemokratie in der Republik'. (Address delivered at the annual conference of the German Social Democratic Party (SPD) in Kiel).
Hilferding, R. 1940, 'State capitalism or totalitarian state economy?', *Socialist Courier* (New York). Reprinted in *Modern Review* (1947).
Hildferding, R. 1941, 'Das historische Problem', *Zeitschrift für Politik* (New series, vol. 1, 1954).
Hindess, B. 1988, *Choice, Rationality and Social Theory* (London: Unwin Hyman).
Hobson, J.A. 1902, *Imperialism: A study* (3rd rev. edn; London: Allen & Unwin, 1938).
Hutchison, T.W. 1981, *The Politics and Philosophy of Economics: Marxians, Keynesians and Austrians* (Oxford: Basil Blackwell).
Hutchison, T.W. 1982, 'Capitalism and its prospects', *Times Literary Supplement*, 5 February.

Janik, A. and Toulmin, S. 1973, *Wittgenstein's Vienna* (New York: Simon & Schuster).

Kraus, K. 1926 (1964), *Die letzten Tage der Menschheit* (Munich: Deutscher Taschenbuch Verlag).
Kuhn, T. 1962, *The Structure of Scientific Revolutions* (2nd edn; Chicago, IL: University of Chicago Press, 1970).

Lakatos, I. and Musgrave, A. (eds) 1970, *Criticism and the Growth of Knowledge* (Cambridge: Cambridge University Press).
Lange, O. and Taylor, F.M. 1938, *On the Economic Theory of Socialism* (Minneapolis, MN: University of Minnesota Press).
Larrain, J. 1986, *A Reconstruction of Historical Materialism* (London: Allen & Unwin).
Larrain, J. 1989, *Theories of Development* (Oxford: Polity/Blackwell).
Lenin, V.I. 1916, *Imperialism, the Highest Stage of Capitalism* (Moscow: Foreign Languages Publishing House, 1947).
Lichtheim, G. 1971, *Imperialism* (New York: Praeger).

Lowit, T. 1962, 'Marx et le mouvement coopératif', *Cahiers de l'Institut de science économique appliquée*, series 129, 'Etudes de Marxologie'.
Löwith, K. 1932, *Max Weber and Karl Marx* (London: Allen & Unwin, 1982).
Lukes, S. 1973, *Individualism* (Oxford: Basil Blackwell).
Luxemburg, R. 1913, *The Accumulation of Capital* (London: Routledge & Kegan Paul, 1951).
Machlup, F. 1951, 'Schumpeter's economic methodology', in Harris, S.E. (ed.) 1951.
Macpherson, C.B. 1962, *The Political Theory of Possessive Individualism* (Oxford: Oxford University Press).
Maddison, A. 1982, *Phases of Capitalist Development* (Oxford and New York: Oxford University Press).
Maddison, A. 1991, *Dynamic Forces in Capitalist Development* (Oxford: Oxford University Press).
Mandel, E. 1980, *Long Waves of Capitalist Development* (Cambridge: Cambridge University Press).
Mandel, E. 1991, 'Long waves', in Bottomore, T. (ed.) 1991b.
Marshall, G. 1982, *In Search of the Spirit of Capitalism* (London: Hutchinson).
Marshall, T.H. 1950, *Citizenship and Social Class* (reprinted in Marshall, T.H. and Bottomore, T. 1992).
Marshall, T.H. and Bottomore, T. 1992, *Citizenship and Social Class* (London: Pluto Press).
Martinez-Alier, J. 1987, *Ecological Economics* (Oxford: Blackwell).
Marx, K. 1857–8, *Grundrisse* (Harmondsworth: Penguin Books, 1973).
Marx, K. 1859, *A Contribution to the Critique of Political Economy*.
Marx, K. 1867, 1885, 1894, *Capital*, 3 vols.
Marx, K. 1865, *Value, Price and Profit* (London: Swan Sonnenschein).
Marx, K. and Engels, F. 1845–6, *German Ideology*.
Marx, K. and Engels, F. 1848, *Communist Manifesto*.
Masterman, M. 1970, 'The nature of a paradigm', in Lakatos, I. and Musgrave, A. (eds) 1970.
Menger, C. 1871, *Grundriss der Volkswirtschaftslehre* (English trans. *Principles of Economics*. New York and London: New York University Press, 1981).
Menger, C. 1883, *Investigations into the Method of the Social Sciences with Special Reference to Economics* (New York: New York University Press, 1985).
Michels, R. 1911, *Political Parties* (Glencoe, IL: Free Press, 1949).
Milford, K. 1990, 'Menger's methodology', in Caldwell, B.J. (ed.) 1990.
Mill, J.S. 1865, *Auguste Comte and Positivism* (Ann Arbor, MI: University of Michigan Press, 1961).

Mills, C.W. 1951, *White Collar* (New York: Oxford University Press).
Mises, L. von 1920, 'Economic calculation in the socialist commonwealth', in Hayek, F.A. (ed.) 1935.
Mises, L. von 1922, *Socialism: An economic and sociological analysis* (London: Jonathan Cape, 1936).
Mises, L. von 1978, *Erinnerungen* (English version under the title *Notes and Recollections*. South Holland, IPP: Libertarian Press).
Mommsen, W.J. 1959, *Max Weber und die deutsche Politik 1890–1920* (Tübingen: J.C.B. Mohr (Paul Siebeck)).
Mommsen, W.J. 1974, *The Age of Bureaucracy: Perspectives on the political sociology of Max Weber* (Oxford: Basil Blackwell).
Mozetič, G. 1985, 'Ein unzeitgemässer Soziologe: Ludwig Gumplowicz', *Kölner Zeitschrift für Soziologie und Sozialpsychologie*, 37, pp. 621–47.
Mozetič, G. 1987, *Die Gesellschaftstheorie des Austromarxismus* (Darmstadt: Wissenschaftliche Buchgesellschaft).
Musgrave, R.A. 1988, 'Discussion', in Hanusch, H. (ed.) 1988, pp. 273–8).
Musil, R. 1930 (1953), *The Man Without Qualities*, vol. I (London: Secker & Warburg).

Neurath, O. 1919, *Through the War Economy to the Natural Economy*, in Neurath, O. 1973.
Neurath, O. 1920, Lecture on experiences of socialization in Bavaria, in Neurath, O. 1973.
Neurath, O. 1931, *Empirical Sociology*, in Neurath, O. 1973.
Neurath, O. 1973, *Empiricism and Sociology*, ed. by M. Neurath and R.S. Cohen (Dordrecht: D. Reidel).
Nimni, E. 1991, *Marxism and Nationalism* (London: Pluto Press).

Offe, C. 1984, *Contradictions of the Welfare State* (Cambridge, Mass.: MIT Press).

Parsons, T. 1951, *The Social System* (New York: Free Press).
Peukert, D.J.K. 1991, *The Weimar Republic: The crisis of classical modernity* (London: Allen Lane).
Popper, K.R. 1934, *The Logic of Scientific Discovery* (London: Hutchinson, 1959).
Popper, K.R. 1963, *Conjectures and Refutations* (London: Routledge & Kegan Paul).
Postan, M.M. 1967, *Economic History of Western Europe, 1945–64* (London: Methuen).
Prychitko, D.L. 1990, 'Claus Offe's theory of the welfare state', *Critical Review*, vol. 4, no. 4, pp. 619–32.

Pulzer, P. 1986, 'Liberalismus, Antisemitismus und Juden im Wien der Jahrhundertwende', in Berner, P. *et al.* (eds) 1986.
Reijnders, J. 1990, *Long Waves in Economic Development* (Aldershot: Edward Elgar).
Renner, K. 1916, 'Probleme des Marxismus', *Der Kampf*, vol. 9.
Renner, K. 1917, *Marxismus, Krieg und Internationale* (Stuttgart: J.H.W. Dietz).
Renner, K. 1921, 'Demokratie und Rätesystem', *Der Kampf*, vol. 14, pp. 54–67 (English trans. in Bottomore, T. and Goode, P. 1978).
Ritzel, G. 1951, *Schmoller versus Menger* (Offenbach: Bollwerk-Verlag).
Ruttan, V. 1959, 'Usher and Schumpeter on invention, innovation, and technological change', *Quarterly Journal of Economics*, no. 73, pp. 596–606.
Schlatter, R. 1951, *Private Property: The history of an idea* (London: Allen & Unwin).
Schorske, C.E. 1980, *Fin-de-siècle Vienna: Politics and culture* (London: Weidenfeld & Nicolson).
Schumpeter, J.A. 1906, 'Über die mathematische Methode der theoretischen Ökonomie', *Zeitschrift für Volkswirtschaft, Sozialpolitik und Verwaltung*, XV, pp. 30–49.
Schumpeter, J.A. 1908, *Das Wesen und der Hauptinhalt der theoretischen Nationalökonomie* (Munich and Leipzig: Duncker & Humblot).
Schumpeter, J.A. 1911, *The Theory of Economic Development* (rev. edn 1926; English edn Cambridge, MA: Harvard University Press, 1934; Japanese edn 1937).
Schumpeter, J.A. 1914a, 'Die "positive" Methode in der Nationalökonomie', *Deutsche Literaturzeitung*, XXXV.
Schumpeter, J.A. 1914b, *Economic Doctrine and Method* (London: Allen & Unwin, 1954).
Schumpeter, J.A. 1918, *Die Krise des Steuerstaats* (Graz und Leipzig: Leuschner & Lubensky).
Schumpeter, J. A. 1919, 'The sociology of imperialisms' (English edn ed. P.M. Sweezy, *Imperialism and Social Classes*, Oxford: Basil Blackwell, 1951).
Schumpeter, J.A. 1920/21, 'Sozialistische Möglichkeiten von heute', *Archiv für Sozialwissenschaft und Sozialpolitik*, vol. 48, pp. 305–60. Reprinted in *Aufsätze zur ökonomischen Theorie* (Tübingen: J.C.B. Mohr (Paul Siebeck), 1952).
Schumpeter, J.A. 1921, 'Carl Menger', in Schumpeter, J.A, 1952.
Schumpeter, J.A. 1927a, 'Friedrich von Wieser', in Schumpeter, J.A. 1952.
Schumpeter, J.A. 1927b, 'Social classes in an ethnically homogeneous

environment' (English edn, ed. P.M. Sweezy, *Imperialism and Social Classes*, Oxford: Basil Blackwell, 1951).
Schumpeter, J.A. 1928a, 'Erbschaftssteuer', *Der deutsche Volkswirt*, vol. 3, pp. 110–14.
Schumpeter, J.A. 1928b, 'The instability of capitalism', *Economic Journal*, vol. 38, pp. 361–8. Reprinted in Schumpeter, 1951.
Schumpeter, J.A. 1929, 'Das soziale Antlitz des deutschen Reiches', *Bonner Mitteilungen*, no. 1, pp. 1–12.
Schumpeter, J.A. 1939, *Business Cycles: A theoretical, historical and statistical analysis of the capitalist process* (New York and London: McGraw-Hill).
Schumpeter, J.A. 1942, *Capitalism, Socialism and Democracy* (6th edn London: Allen & Unwin, 1987).
Schumpeter, J.A. 1946a, 'John Maynard Keynes', in Schumpeter, J.A. 1952.
Schumpeter, J.A. 1946b, 'Capitalism', in Schumpeter, J.A. 1951.
Schumpeter, J.A. 1949, 'Vilfredo Pareto', in Schumpeter, J.A. 1952.
Schumpeter, J.A. 1951, *Essays on Economic Topics*, ed. R.V. Clemence (Port Washington, NY: Kennikat Press).
Schumpeter, J.A. 1952, *Ten Great Economists* (London: Allen & Unwin).
Schumpeter, J.A. 1953, *Aufsätze zür Soziologie* (Tübingen: J.C.B. Mohr (Paul Siebeck)).
Schumpeter, J.A. 1954, *History of Economic Analysis* (London: Allen & Unwin).
Schumpeter, J.A. 1970, *Das Wesen des Geldes*, ed. F.K. Mann (Göttingen: Vandenhoecht & Ruprecht).
Schumpeter, J.A. 1985, *Aufsätze zur Wirtschaftspolitik*, ed. W. Stolper and C. Seidl (Tübingen: J.C.B. Mohr (Paul Siebeck)).
Scott, J. 1982, *The Upper Classes: Property and Privilege in Britain* (London: Macmillan).
Scott, J. 1991, *Who Rules Britain?* (Oxford: Polity/Blackwell).
Seidl, C. (ed.) 1984, *Lectures on Schumpeterian Economics* (Berlin: Springer-Verlag).
Shaw, W.H. 1978, *Marx's Theory of History* (London: Hutchinson).
Simiand, F. 1912, *La méthode positive en science économique* (Paris: Félix Alcan).
Simmel, G. 1907, *The Philosophy of Money* (London: Routledge & Kegan Paul, 1978).
Simmel, G. 1908, 'How is society possible?', in Wolff, K.H. (ed.), *Georg Simmel 1858–1918* (Columbus, OH: Ohio State University Press, 1959).
Smithies, A. 1951, 'Memorial: Joseph Alois Schumpeter, 1883–1950', in Harris, S.E. (ed.) 1951.

Streissler, E. 1982, 'Schumpeter's Vienna and the role of credit in innovation', in Frisch, H. (ed.), *Schumpeterian Economics* (Eastbourne and New York: Praeger).

Swedberg, R. 1987, 'The tradition of economic sociology, 1800s–1960s', *Current Sociology*, 35, 1, pp. 11–62.

Swedberg, R. 1991, *Joseph A. Schumpeter: His life and work* (Oxford: Polity/Blackwell).

Sweezy, P.M. (ed.) 1951, *Imperialism and Social Classes* (Oxford: Basil Blackwell).

Swoboda, P. 1984, 'Schumpeter's entrepreneur in modern economic theory', in Seidl, C. (ed.) 1984.

Tichy, G. 1984, 'Schumpeter's Business Cycle Theory. Its importance for our time', in Seidl, C. (ed.) 1984.

Veblen, T. 1915, *Imperial Germany and the Industrial Revolution* (New York: Augustus M. Kelley, 1964).

Weber, M. 1904, ' "Objectivity" in social science and social policy', in Weber, M. 1949.

Weber, M. 1904–5, *The Protestant Ethic and the Spirit of Capitalism* (London: Allen & Unwin, 1976).

Weber, M. 1918a, 'Parliament and government in a reconstructed Germany' (English trans. as appendix to Weber, M. 1921).

Weber, M. 1918b, 'Socialism' (English trans. in Eldridge, J.E.T. (ed.), *Max Weber: The interpretation of social reality* (London: Michael Joseph, 1970), pp. 191–219).

Weber, M. 1919, 'Politics as a vocation' (English trans. in Gerth, H.H. and Mills, C.W. (eds), *From Max Weber* (London: Routledge & Kegan Paul, 1947), pp. 77–128).

Weber, M. 1921, *Economy and Society* (New York: Bedminster Press, 1968).

Weber, M. 1923, *General Economic History* (New York: Collier Books, 1961).

Weber, M. 1949, *The Methodology of the Social Sciences* (trans. and ed. by E.A. Shils and H.A. Finch (New York: Free Press)).

Weber, M. 1971, *Gesammelte politische Schriften* (3rd edn Tübingen: J.C.B. Mohr).

Wieser, F. von 1893, *Natural Value* (London: Macmillan).

Wieser, F. von 1929, *Gesammelte Abhandlungen*, ed. F.A. Hayek (Tübingen: J.C.B. Mohr).

Winslow, E.M. 1948, *The Pattern of Imperialism: A study in the theories of power* (New York: Columbia University Press).

Yeo, S. 1991, 'Cooperative association', in Bottomore, T. (ed.) 1991b

INDEX

Adler, M., 12, 24, 27, 110, 134
Agassi, J., 27
Amsden, A.H., 50
anti-Semitism, 11
Aron, R., 48, 59, 125
Austrian Republic, Schumpeter as Secretary of the Treasury, 13, 34
Austrian school of economics, 2, 7, 17, 31, 35
Austro-Marxism, 2, 9, 13, 18, 24, 78, 109

banks, 90
Barea, I., 5
Barone, E., 110
Bauer, O., 9, 11, 12, 36, 43, 44, 45, 88, 97, 109
Berner, P., 11
Bernstein, E., 55
Bhaskar, R., 25
Böhm-Bawerk, E. von, 7, 8, 9
Boltzmann, L. E., 6
bourgeoisie, 54, 80, 92–3, 114, 120, 121
Britain, 46, 69, 105, 130
Brubaker, R., 126
Brym, R.J., 94

Bukharin, N., 45
bureaucracy, 91, 103, 122

capitalism, 47, 77, 78, 85, 90, 93, 100, 102, 118, 119, 124, 127, 128–9, 130
  breakdown of, 88–9, 98, 104, 105, 114
  competitive, 39
  instability of, 39, 41, 131
  organized, 39, 40, 41, 44, 79, 91, 117
  rise of, 76, 118
causality, 25, 32, 33, 75
circular flow, 19, 29, 31
citizenship, 111, 129
class, 5, 50–4, 87, 93, 98, 102, 106, 113–4, 124
class structure, 55, 58, 87
combinations, 31–2
commodity, 20
competition, 90, 99, 116, 121
Comte, A., 59, 125
cooperation, 116
corporations, 88, 90, 92, 97, 116, 117
corporatism, 65, 130
credit, 42, 92

148 *Index*

Csaky, M., 11

democracy, 37–8, 107–10, 117, 123
dynamic analysis, 17

Eastern Europe, 105, 106, 110, 129, 131
economic calculation, 57, 103, 122
economic cycles (*see* also, long waves), 32–3, 62–84, 115, 130
economic development, 28–44, 132–3
economic history, 1, 16, 113
economic interpretation of history, 41, 86, 112–13, 124, 127, 135
economic sociology, 2, 13, 112, 134
elite, 53
empiricism, 22–3
Engels, F., 30, 113
entrepreneur, 10, 32–3, 37, 72–3, 75–6, 80, 81, 91–2, 106
  collective, 72, 73, 97
  decline of, 34, 91, 116
environment, 133
equilibrium analysis, 10, 15, 17, 40, 63, 78, 83

fascism, 49, 60
Fellner, W., 102
firm, theory of the, 80, 82
Fordism, 43, 65
France, 46
Franks, 46, 86
Freeman, C., 71
functionalism, 23, 27

Gelderen, J. van, 83
German Commission on Socialization, 13, 34, 43, 108

Germany, 43, 49–50, 55–7, 87, 133
Godelier, M., 24
Goldscheid, R., 54
Gordon, D.M., 67, 68
Gulick, C.A., 36, 43
Gumplowicz, L., 51, 59, 60

Habsburg Empire, 5, 11, 12
Haddon, A.C., 51
'halfway house', 99, 106, 117, 128, 130
Heertje, A., 91
Heller, E., 6
Hertz, H., 6
Hilferding, R., 9, 12, 13, 18, 20, 24, 30, 34, 37, 38, 42, 43, 44, 45, 47, 48, 57, 72, 88, 89, 90, 91, 102, 104, 109, 116, 117, 134, 135
Hindess, B., 27
historical school, 2, 15
history, 4, 41
Hitler, Adolf, 47
Hobson, J.A., 45
Hungary, 43
Hutchison, T.W., 3

ideal type, 65, 119, 121
ideology, 22, 95
imperialism, 45–50, 72, 88–9
  social, 48–9, 89
individual, 19, 52, 54, 120
individualism, 81, 96–7
industrial society, 59, 125–6
innovation, 40, 63–4, 71, 73, 77, 81, 91–2
intellectuals, 56, 93–4, 98
invention, 63–4, 70, 81

Janik, A., 6, 10
Japan, 133
Juglar, C., 32, 43, 64, 66

Kéler, S. von, 7
Keynes, J.M., 3, 30, 65
Kitchin, J., 64, 66
Kondratiev, N.D., 65, 66, 69, 83
Kraus, K., 5
Kuhn, T., 27

Lakatos, I., 27
Lange, O., 58, 110
language, 6
laws, 8
leadership, 54, 78, 123
Lederer, E., 9
Lenin, V.I., 45
Lichtheim, G., 49
long waves (*see* also, economic cycles), 64–5, 66–72, 74, 79–80, 115
Luxemburg, R., 45

Machlup, F., 16
Maddison, A., 66, 67, 110
Mandel, E., 67, 68–9, 70, 74, 83
Mann, F.K., 61
marginal utility theory, 7, 13, 17, 28
Marshall, A., 17
Marshall Plan, 105
Marshall, T.H., 95, 110, 111
Marx, K., 24, 29, 30, 31, 34, 37, 63, 70, 71, 74, 76, 78, 79, 83–4, 85–9, 98, 102, 110, 112, 113, 115, 116, 119, 123, 127, 134
Marxism, 3, 17, 35, 67, 80, 88–9, 114, 118, 125
Masterman, M., 21, 31
mathematical methods, 15, 16
Mauthner, F., 6
Menger, C., 7, 8, 12, 15, 19, 23–4, 31
Methodenstreit, 10, 15, 16, 26
methodological individualism, 10, 19, 25, 27, 51

methodological tolerance, 16, 17
methodology, 16–17, 25, 26
Michels, R., 110
middle class, 129
militarism, 48
Mill, J.S., 27
Mills, C.W., 96
Mises, L. von, 9, 12, 103
mixed economy, 104, 130
model, 18, 23, 65, 121
modernization, 126–7
money, 57–8
Mozetic, G., 12, 13
Musgrave, A., 27
Musgrave, R. A., 60, 131
Musil, R., 5, 6, 11

nation state, 97, 120–1, 124
nationalism, 2, 5, 11, 48, 97
neo-Kantianism, 5
Neurath, O., 9, 13, 22, 43, 122
Nietzsche, F., 59

Offe, C., 61

paradigm, 21, 26, 30, 35
Pareto, V., 41, 53, 60, 76, 95, 107, 111
Parsons, T., 126
Parvus (Helphand, A.), 83
peasantry, 55
Peukert, D., 44, 126
philosophy of science, 15
planning, 44, 117, 132
Popper, K., 27
positivism, 5, 8, 21–2, 27
Postan, M.M., 104
private property, 93, 95–6
privatization, 96, 130, 132
production, 41
production function, 64
protectionism, 47, 48, 88
Protestant ethic, 118, 120
Prychitko, D.L., 60

public ownership, 132

race, 51
rational choice, 27
rationality, 60, 119, 120
rationalization, 37, 43, 95, 119, 120, 125
realism, 25
Reijnders, J., 66, 69, 83
Renner, K., 11, 44, 48, 55, 97, 103
Robinson, J., 2
Russia, 46
Ruttan, V., 71

Saint-Simon, H. de, 59, 125
Schlatter, R., 95
Schmoller, G., 9
Schorske, C.E., 11
Schumpeter, Mrs, 11
scientific revolutions, 27
Seidl, C., 11
Simiand, F., 23
Simmel, G., 27, 51, 57, 61
Smithies, A., 7
social mobility, 87
socialism, 2, 5, 36–9, 85, 87, 101–6, 117, 121–2, 124–5, 127, 128, 131
socialization, 20, 36–8, 43, 91, 97, 101, 103, 115–6, 134
socialized humanity, 134
sociology, 2, 58
Sombart, W., 9, 76
Spencer, H., 59, 125
Spiethoff, A.A.K., 32
state intervention, 44, 65, 80, 117
static analysis, 17, 29, 42
statistics, 1, 15
Streissler, E., 90
structuralism, 24
Swedberg, R., 11, 136
Sweezy, P., 44
Swoboda, P., 90

tax state, 54–5, 130–1
Taylor, F.M., 110
Taylorism, 43, 56
technology, 70–1, 73, 114
theory, 1–2, 16, 19, 23
Third World, 126, 133
Tichy, G., 71
Tolstoy, L., 11
totalitarianism, 105, 117
Toulmin, S., 6, 11
Tugan-Baranowsky, M.I., 83

unemployment, 88, 98
USA, 133
USSR, 43, 105, 107

value,
  Austrian theory of, 7
  labour theory of, 12, 20, 87–8
values, 11
  capitalist, 94–7, 99
Veblen, T., 48, 59
Vienna, 5–6, 11
Vienna Circle, 6
vision, 22, 30, 35, 70, 110, 120

wage labour, 99
Walras, L., 15, 63
war, effects on the economy, 103–4
warrior nations, 46
Weber, M., 2, 3, 9, 13, 37, 41, 52, 57, 65, 76, 97, 100, 104, 107, 109, 110, 111, 118, 119–23, 124, 125, 126, 127, 128, 135
welfare state, 104, 130, 131
Wieser, F. von, 7, 8, 10, 41, 44
Winslow, E.M., 48, 60
Wittgenstein, L., 6, 11
workers' councils, 38, 43, 108, 111
working class, 56, 60, 87, 88, 89, 129